AAT
DEVOLVED ASSESSMENT KIT

Technician Unit 16

Evaluating Activities

In this August 2000 edition

- The **Unit 16 standards in full**, including latest (2000) guidance from the AAT
- Expanded bank of **practice activities** to reinforce learning
- **Practice Devolved Assessments** to bring you up to speed on certain areas of the Standards
- **Trial Run Devolved Assessments** covering all Elements of Competence for the Unit
- The **AAT's Sample Simulation** for the Unit
- **Key terms highlighted** in answers

All Simulations and Assessments have **full answers** included in this Kit.

FOR 2000 AND 2001 DEVOLVED ASSESSMENTS

BPP Publishing
August 2000

First edition 1998
Third edition August 2000

ISBN 0 7517 6247 4 (previous edition 0 7517 6177 X)

British Library Cataloguing-in-Publication Data
A catalogue record for this book
is available from the British Library

Published by

BPP Publishing Limited
Aldine House, Aldine Place
London W12 8AW

www.bpp.com

Printed in Great Britain by Ashford Colour Press

We are grateful to the Lead Body for Accounting for permission to reproduce
extracts from the Standards of Competence for Accounting and to the AAT for
permission to reproduce their assessments and simulations.

INTRODUCTION

Contents

ORDER FORM

REVIEW FORM & FREE PRIZE DRAW

HOW TO USE THIS DEVOLVED ASSESSMENT KIT

Aims of this Devolved Assessment Kit

> To provide the knowledge and practice to help you succeed in the devolved assessment for Technician Unit 16 *Evaluating Current and Proposed Activities.*

To pass the devolved assessment you need a thorough understanding in all areas covered by the standards of competence.

> To tie in with the other components of the BPP Effective Study Package to ensure you have the best possible chance of success.

Interactive Text

This covers all you need to know for devolved assessment for Unit 16. Icons clearly mark key areas of the text. Numerous activities throughout the text help you practise what you have just learnt.

Devolved Assessment Kit

When you have understood and practised the material in the Interactive Text, you will have the knowledge and experience to tackle this Devolved Assessment Kit for Unit 16. This aims to get you through the devolved assessment, whether in the form of a simulation or workplace assessment. It contains the AAT's Sample Simulation for Unit 16 plus other simulations.

Recommended approach to this Devolved Assessment Kit

- To achieve competence in all units you need to be able to do **everything** specified by the standards. Study the Interactive Text very carefully and do not skip any of it.

- Learning is an **active** process. Do **all** the activities as you work through the Interactive Text so you can be sure you really understand what you have read.

- After you have covered the material in the Interactive Text, work through this **Devolved Assessment Kit**.

- Try the **Practice Activities**. These are short activities, designed to reinforce your learning and to consolidate the practice that you have had doing the activities in the Interactive Text.

- Then attempt the **Practice Devolved Assessments**. They are designed to test your competence in certain key areas of the Standards of Competence, but are not as comprehensive as the ones set by the AAT. They are 'warm-up' exercises, to develop your studies towards the level of full devolved assessment.

- Next do the **Trial Run Devolved Assessments**. Although these are not yet fully at the level you can expect when you do a full devolved assessment, they cover all the performance criteria of the elements indicated.

- Finally try the AAT's **Sample Simulation,** which gives you the clearest idea of what a full assessment will be like.

Introduction

Remember this is a **practical** course.

(a)   Try to relate the material to your experience in the workplace or any other work experience you may have had.

(b)   Try to make as many links as you can to your study of the other units at this level.

UNIT 16 STANDARDS OF COMPETENCE

The structure of the Standards for Unit 16

The unit commences with a statement of the **knowledge and understanding** which underpin competence in the unit's elements.

The unit is then divided into **elements of competence** describing activities which the individual should be able to perform.

Each element includes:

- A set of **performance criteria** which define what constitutes competent performance

- A **range statement** which defines the situations, contexts, methods etc in which competence should be displayed

- **Evidence requirements,** which state that competence must be demonstrated consistently, over an appropriate time scale with evidence of performance being provided from the appropriate sources

- **Sources of evidence,** being suggestions of ways in which you can find evidence to demonstrate that competence

The elements of competence for Unit 16 *Evaluating Current and Proposed Activities* are set out below. Knowledge and understanding required for the Unit as a whole are listed first, followed by the performance criteria, range statements, evidence requirements and sources of evidence for each element. Performance criteria are cross-referenced below to chapters in the Unit 16 Interactive Text.

Unit 16: Evaluating current and proposed activities

What is the unit about?

This unit is about preparing cost estimates for work activity and projects. It involves the analysis of information to identify current costs and future trends. The unit requires cost estimates to be prepared and supported by a clear rationale.

BPP
PUBLISHING

Accounting techniques

- Basic statistical methods: index numbers, time series (Element 16.1)
- Marginal costing, absorption costing, opportunity costs (Elements 16.1 & 16.2)
- Interpretation of cost data, the use of overhead rates (Element 16.1)
- The identification of fixed, variable and semi-fixed costs and their correct use in cost analysis (Element 16.2)
- The identification of relevant costs (Element 16.2)
- The identification of limiting factors (Element 16.2)
- Methods of project appraisal: payback, discounted cash flow methods (NPV and IRR) (Element 16.2)
- Basic principles of risk analysis: Expected Monetary Return (Element 16.2)
- A basic understanding of the tax implications of capital expenditure (capital allowances and their effect on future cash flows) (Element 16.2)

Accounting principles and theory

- Cost behaviour (Elements 16.1 & 16.2)
- The economic basis of pricing policies (Element 16.1)
- The principles of DCF, comparison of different methods (Element 16.2)
- Risk and uncertainty (Element 16.2)

The organisation

- Understanding that the accounting systems of an organisation are affected by its organisational structure, its administrative systems and procedures and the nature of its business transactions (Elements 16.1 & 16.2)
- A knowledge of the sources of information about labour, material and overhead costs (Element 16.1)

Element 16.1 Prepare cost estimates

Performance criteria	Chapters in the Text
1 The extent of the information to be contained within estimates is agreed with those who commission them	8
2 Appropriate staff are consulted about technical aspects and any special features of work activity and projects which impact upon costs	Throughout
3 Current material, labour and other variable costs are identified and future trends assessed	2
4 Estimates account for the effect of possible variations in capacity on fixed overhead rates	2
5 Estimates are prepared in an approved form and presented to the appropriate people within an agreed timescale	1, 8

Range statement

1 Estimates prepared for: price fixing; submitting tenders or quotations; costing proposed activities and projects	8

Evidence requirements

- Competence must be demonstrated consistently, over an appropriate timescale with evidence of performance being provided of providing cost estimates.

Sources of evidence (these are examples of sources of evidence, but candidates and assessors may be able to identify other appropriate sources)

- *Observed performance*, eg
  - Presentations to colleagues relating to cost estimates
  - Meetings and discussions with colleagues relating to the preparation and presentation of cost estimates

- *Work produced by candidate*, eg
  - Cost estimates
  - Costing reports
  - Correspondence relating to the identification and estimation of costs

- *Authenticated testimonies from relevant witnesses*

- *Personal accounts of competence*, eg
  - Report of performance

- *Other sources of evidence to prove competence or knowledge and understanding where it is not apparent from performance*, eg
  - Performance in independent assessment
  - Performance in simulation
  - Responses to verbal questioning

Element 16.2   Recommend ways to improve cost ratios and revenue generation

Performance criteria	Chapters in the Text
1 Information relevant to estimating current and future costs and revenue is identified and used as the basis of analysis	12
2 Critical factors which may affect costs and revenue are analysed using appropriate accounting techniques and clear conclusions are drawn from the analysis	9
3 The views of appropriate specialists are gathered and used to inform analysis and any conclusions drawn	8
4 The assumptions made and the degree of accuracy which exists in conclusions are clearly stated	8
5 Potential options and solutions are identified and evaluated for their contribution to improving cost ratios and revenue generation	6
6 Recommendations to inform decisions are based on clearly stated conclusions drawn from an accurate analysis of all relevant information	8
7 Recommendations are presented to the appropriate people in a clear and concise way and are supported with a clear rationale	8, 12

Range statement

1 Type of decisions: decisions relating to operational activities of the "make or buy" type; decisions relating to strategic planning and future project activity	5
2 Types of information: - internal information: accounting information, technical data, cost estimates - external information: competitor prices, supplier prices, market information	7
3 Techniques related to: the identification of fixed, variable and semi-fixed costs and their correct use in cost analysis; marginal costing; opportunity costs; the identification of limiting factors - methods of project appraisal: payback; discounted cash flow methods NPV and IRR - risk analysis: identifying Expected Monetary Return	1-4, 9, 12
4 Methods of presentation: verbal presentation; written reports	1

Evidence requirements

- Competence must be demonstrated consistently, over an appropriate timescale with evidence of performance being provided of analysis which informs make or buy type decisions and strategic planning decisions.

Element 16.2 Recommend ways to improve cost ratios and revenue generation

Sources of evidence (these are example of sources of evidence, but candidates and assessors may be able to identify other appropriate sources)

- *Observed performance*, eg
  - Meetings held to gather and discuss data and views about current future costs and revenue
  - Presentations relating to potential options and solutions for improving cost ratios and revenue generation

- *Work produced by candidate*, eg
  - Documentation relating to current and future costs and revenue
  - Reports containing analysis conclusions and recommendations
  - Correspondence relating to current and future costs and revenue

- *Authenticated testimonies from relevant witnesses*

- *Personal accounts of competence*, eg
  - Report of performance

- *Other sources of evidence to prove competence or knowledge and understanding where it is not apparent from performance*, eg
  - Reports and working papers
  - Performance in independent assessment
  - Performance in simulation
  - Responses to verbal questioning

BPP PUBLISHING

ASSESSMENT STRATEGY

Unit 16 is assessed by *devolved* assessment.

The theme throughout the unit is decision making in all its facets and the use of relevant techniques and concepts to aid valid decisions. Within decision making, there is a natural division between short-term and long-term decision making and so it seems logical that any assessment should recognise this division. The division into long-term and short-term decision making is also aided by all the concept and techniques being generic. It is therefore suggested that any simulation or other form of devolved assessment should recognise these features. The interrelationships are shown in the table below, which should serve as model for assessment.

	Short-term, operational decision making	Long-term, strategic decision making
Element 16.1	• Marginal costing • Absorption costing • Cost behaviour • Tenders and quotations	• Index numbers • Time series
Element 16.2	• Fixed, variable and semi-variable costs • Relevant and opportunity costs • Limiting factors • Make-or-buy type of decision • Risk analysis	• Payback • NPV and IRR • Capital allowance and their effect on cash flows

Devolved assessment

Devolved assessment is a means of collecting evidence of your ability to carry out **practical activities** and to **operate effectively in the conditions of the workplace** to the standards required. Evidence may be collected at your place of work or at an Approved Assessment Centre by means of simulations of workplace activity, or by a combination of these methods.

If the Approved Assessment Centre is a **workplace**, you may be observed carrying out accounting activities as part of your normal work routine. You should collect documentary evidence of the work you have done, or contributed to, in an **accounting portfolio**. Evidence collected in a portfolio can be assessed in addition to observed performance or where it is not possible to assess by observation.

Where the Approved Assessment Centre is a **college or training organisation**, devolved assessment will be by means of a combination of the following.

• Documentary evidence of activities carried out at the workplace, collected by you in an **accounting portfolio**.

• Realistic **simulations** of workplace activities. These simulations may take the form of case studies and in-tray exercises and involve the use of primary documents and reference sources.

• **Projects and assignments** designed to assess the Standards of Competence.

If you are unable to provide workplace evidence you will be able to complete the assessment requirements by the alternative methods listed above.

Below is a list of **possible methods for assessing accounting competence.**

Assessment method	Suitable for assessing
Performance of an accounting task either in the workplace or by simulation: eg preparing and processing documents, posting entries, making adjustments, balancing, calculating, analysing information etc by manual or computerised processes	**Basic task competence**. Adding supplementary oral questioning may help to draw out underpinning knowledge and understanding and highlight your ability to deal with contingencies and unexpected occurrences.
General case studies. These are broader than simulations. They include more background information about the system and business environment.	Ability to **analyse a system** and suggest ways of modifying it. It could take the form of a written report, with or without the addition of oral or written questions.
Accounting problems/cases: eg a list of balances that require adjustments and the preparation of final accounts	Understanding of the **general principles of accounting** as applied to a particular case or topic
Preparation of flowcharts/diagrams. To illustrate an actual (or simulated) accounting procedure	**Understanding of the logic** behind a procedure, of controls, and of relationships between departments and procedures. Questions on the flow chart or diagram can provide evidence of underpinning knowledge and understanding.
Interpretation of accounting information from an actual or simulated situation. The assessment could include non-financial information and written or oral questioning.	**Interpretative competence**
Preparation of written reports on an actual or simulated situation	**Written communication skills**
Analysis of critical incidents, problems encountered, achievements	Your ability to handle **contingencies**
Listing of likely errors eg preparing a list of the main types of errors likely to occur in an actual or simulated procedure	Appreciation of the range of **contingencies** likely to be encountered. Oral or written questioning would be a useful supplement to the list.
Outlining the organisation's policies, guidelines and regulations	Performance criteria relating to these aspects of competence. It also provides evidence of competence in **researching information**.
Objective tests and short-answer questions	**Specific knowledge**
In-tray exercises	Your **task-management ability** as well as technical competence.
Supervisors' reports	**General job competence**, personal effectiveness, reliability, accuracy, and time management. Reports need to be related specifically to the Standards of Competence.
Analysis of work logbooks/diaries	**Personal effectiveness**, time management etc. It may usefully be supplemented with oral questioning.

BPP PUBLISHING

Assessment method	Suitable for assessing
Formal written answers to questions	Knowledge and understanding of the **general accounting environment** and its impact on particular units of competence
Oral questioning	**Knowledge and understanding** across the range of competence including organisational procedures, methods of dealing with unusual cases, contingencies and so on. It is often used in conjunction with other methods.

MATHEMATICAL TABLES

PRESENT VALUE TABLE

Present value of $1 = (1+r)^{-n}$ where r = discount rate, n = number of periods until payment

This table shows the present value of £1 per annum, receivable or payable at the end of *n* years.

Periods					Discount rates (r)					
(n)	1%	2%	3%	4%	5%	6%	7%	8%	9%	10%
1	0.990	0.980	0.971	0.962	0.952	0.943	0.935	0.926	0.917	0.909
2	0.980	0.961	0.943	0.925	0.907	0.890	0.873	0.857	0.842	0.826
3	0.971	0.942	0.915	0.889	0.864	0.840	0.816	0.794	0.772	0.751
4	0.961	0.924	0.888	0.855	0.823	0.792	0.763	0.735	0.708	0.683
5	0.951	0.906	0.863	0.822	0.784	0.747	0.713	0.681	0.650	0.621
6	0.942	0.888	0.837	0.790	0.746	0.705	0.666	0.630	0.596	0.564
7	0.933	0.871	0.813	0.760	0.711	0.665	0.623	0.583	0.547	0.513
8	0.923	0.853	0.789	0.731	0.677	0.627	0.582	0.540	0.502	0.467
9	0.914	0.837	0.766	0.703	0.645	0.592	0.544	0.500	0.460	0.424
10	0.905	0.820	0.744	0.676	0.614	0.558	0.508	0.463	0.422	0.386
11	0.896	0.804	0.722	0.650	0.585	0.527	0.475	0.429	0.388	0.350
12	0.887	0.788	0.701	0.625	0.557	0.497	0.444	0.397	0.356	0.319
13	0.879	0.773	0.681	0.601	0.530	0.469	0.415	0.368	0.326	0.290
14	0.870	0.758	0.661	0.577	0.505	0.442	0.388	0.340	0.299	0.263
15	0.861	0.743	0.642	0.555	0.481	0.417	0.362	0.315	0.275	0.239

	11%	12%	13%	14%	15%	16%	17%	18%	19%	20%
1	0.901	0.893	0.885	0.877	0.870	0.862	0.855	0.847	0.840	0.833
2	0.812	0.797	0.783	0.769	0.756	0.743	0.731	0.718	0.706	0.694
3	0.731	0.712	0.693	0.675	0.658	0.641	0.624	0.609	0.593	0.579
4	0.659	0.636	0.613	0.592	0.572	0.552	0.534	0.516	0.499	0.482
5	0.593	0.567	0.543	0.519	0.497	0.476	0.456	0.437	0.419	0.402
6	0.535	0.507	0.480	0.456	0.432	0.410	0.390	0.370	0.352	0.335
7	0.482	0.452	0.425	0.400	0.376	0.354	0.333	0.314	0.296	0.279
8	0.434	0.404	0.376	0.351	0.327	0.305	0.285	0.266	0.249	0.233
9	0.391	0.361	0.333	0.308	0.284	0.263	0.243	0.225	0.209	0.194
10	0.352	0.322	0.295	0.270	0.247	0.227	0.208	0.191	0.176	0.162
11	0.317	0.287	0.261	0.237	0.215	0.195	0.178	0.162	0.148	0.135
12	0.286	0.257	0.231	0.208	0.187	0.168	0.152	0.137	0.124	0.112
13	0.258	0.229	0.204	0.182	0.163	0.145	0.130	0.116	0.104	0.093
14	0.232	0.205	0.181	0.160	0.141	0.125	0.111	0.099	0.088	0.078
15	0.209	0.183	0.160	0.140	0.123	0.108	0.095	0.084	0.074	0.065

ANNUITY TABLE

Present value of an annuity of 1 ie $\dfrac{1-(1+r)^{-n}}{r}$

where r = discount rate

n = number of periods

Periods	Discount rates (r)									
(n)	1%	2%	3%	4%	5%	6%	7%	8%	9%	10%
1	0.990	0.980	0.971	0.962	0.952	0.943	0.935	0.926	0.917	0.909
2	1.970	1.942	1.913	1.886	1.859	1.833	1.808	1.783	1.759	1.736
3	2.941	2.884	2.829	2.775	2.723	2.673	2.624	2.577	2.531	2.487
4	3.902	3.808	3.717	3.630	3.546	3.465	3.387	3.312	3.240	3.170
5	4.853	4.713	4.580	4.452	4.329	4.212	4.100	3.993	3.890	3.791
6	5.795	5.601	5.417	5.242	5.076	4.917	4.767	4.623	4.486	4.355
7	6.728	6.472	6.230	6.002	5.786	5.582	5.389	5.206	5.033	4.868
8	7.652	7.325	7.020	6.733	6.463	6.210	5.971	5.747	5.535	5.335
9	8.566	8.162	7.786	7.435	7.108	6.802	6.515	6.247	5.995	5.759
10	9.471	8.983	8.530	8.111	7.722	7.360	7.024	6.710	6.418	6.145
11	10.37	9.787	9.253	8.760	8.306	7.887	7.499	7.139	6.805	6.495
12	11.26	10.58	9.954	9.385	8.863	8.384	7.943	7.536	7.161	6.814
13	12.13	11.35	10.63	9.986	9.394	8.853	8.358	7.904	7.487	7.103
14	13.00	12.11	11.30	10.56	9.899	9.295	8.745	8.244	7.786	7.367
15	13.87	12.85	11.94	11.12	10.38	9.712	9.108	8.559	8.061	7.606

	11%	12%	13%	14%	15%	16%	17%	18%	19%	20%
1	0.901	0.893	0.885	0.877	0.870	0.862	0.855	0.847	0.840	0.833
2	1.713	1.690	1.668	1.647	1.626	1.605	1.585	1.566	1.547	1.528
3	2.444	2.402	2.361	2.322	2.283	2.246	2.210	2.174	2.140	2.106
4	3.102	3.037	2.974	2.914	2.855	2.798	2.743	2.690	2.639	2.589
5	3.696	3.605	3.517	3.433	3.352	3.274	3.199	3.127	3.058	2.991
6	4.231	4.111	3.998	3.889	3.784	3.685	3.589	3.498	3.410	3.326
7	4.712	4.564	4.423	4.288	4.160	4.039	3.922	3.812	3.706	3.605
8	5.146	4.968	4.799	4.639	4.487	4.344	4.207	4.078	3.954	3.837
9	5.537	5.328	5.132	4.946	4.772	4.607	4.451	4.303	4.163	4.031
10	5.889	5.650	5.426	5.216	5.019	4.833	4.659	4.494	4.339	4.192
11	6.207	5.938	5.687	5.453	5.234	5.029	4.836	4.656	4.486	4.327
12	6.492	6.194	5.918	5.660	5.421	5.197	4.988	4.793	4.611	4.439
13	6.750	6.424	6.122	5.842	5.583	5.342	5.118	4.910	4.715	4.533
14	6.982	6.628	6.302	6.002	5.724	5.468	5.229	5.008	4.802	4.611
15	7.191	6.811	6.462	6.142	5.847	5.575	5.324	5.092	4.876	4.675

Practice activities

1   ROBERT MOTHERWELL (44 mins)

Robert Motherwell operates a small workshop which makes two products, a garden seat and a child's swing. The products are marketed by an agent who takes all units produced and receives a commission of 20% of the wholesale selling price. Robert estimates that his current costs per unit of production are as follows.

	Garden seat £ per unit	*Child's swing* £ per unit
Raw materials	2	8
Bought-out components	8	1
Labour	3	9
Production overheads (variable)	1	3
General overheads (fixed)	4	4
Wholesale selling price	30	40
Current annual production	2,000 units	2,000 units

Robert estimates that production overheads are incurred at the rate of 33$\frac{1}{3}$% of labour costs. General overheads include depreciation, insurance, rates, professional fees and administrative costs. He estimates that these amount to £16,000 in total per annum, and for costing purposes these costs are apportioned equally between all units of production.

Robert is thinking of making a number of changes in the way in which he runs his business. He asks you, as his financial adviser, to examine each of the following proposals in turn and give your advice. Treat each proposal as a separate item.

(a) *Proposal 1*

Robert is considering making some of the bought-out components for the garden seat in his own workshop. He has sufficient spare capacity to do this. He estimates that he will save 75% of the cost of bought-out components, but that raw material cost and labour costs will double.

Task

Would it be worth making the bought-out components in the workshop? Give reasons for your answer.   (10 mins)

(b) *Proposal 2*

Robert believes that the workshop could make more profit if he undertook the marketing of his products himself rather than employing an agent. He estimates that doing the work himself would cost an additional £5,000 per annum plus £4.00 per unit sold. Sales would not be affected.

Task

Would it be more profitable for Robert to do his own marketing? Give reasons for your answer.   (12 mins)

(c) *Proposal 3*

Robert is considering buying a new machine which, it is hoped, should speed up production of both the swing and the seat. This would involve scrapping much of the existing equipment. Robert has sent you a note in which he says, 'I think that it would be worthwhile to buy the new machine, were it not for the depreciation on the old machine, which we will still have to show in the accounts because, when we bought it three years ago, we agreed to write it off over five years'.

Task

Is Robert correct in his assumption? Write a brief note in reply to him.   (11 mins)

(d) *Proposal 4*

At the moment Robert produces 4,000 units per annum (2,000 swings and 2,000 garden seats). He wishes to expand production to 6,000 units over the next year, but does not want to increase his labour costs significantly beyond the £24,000 which he currently spends. Which of the two products should he market most strongly to achieve a product mix which will give him the most profit? Note that all other costs apart from labour could be increased.

Task

Give your recommendation, with reasons, in brief note form. (11 mins)

2 JZ COMPANY (45 mins)

The budget for JZ company for next year is for 20,000 units of product Z to be produced each month. The standard cost of each unit is as follows.

	£
Direct material	4.50
Direct labour	1.50
Fixed overhead	3.00
	9.00

The standard selling price is £15.00

Information for the first two months of the year

	Month 1	Month 2
Actual sales	18,000	22,000
Actual production (as budgeted)	20,000	20,000

Tasks

(a) Prepare profit and loss accounts for month 1 and month 2 assuming the firm uses the following costing systems.

    (i) Marginal costing

    (ii) Full or total absorption costing (15 mins)

(b) Calculate the stock valuation under each of the two costing methods. (6 mins)

(c) In making its products the JZ Company uses a special component X which could be purchased from an outside firm.

The company accountant has calculated that the 40,000 components needed have the following unit costs if manufactured.

	£
Direct material	1.20
Direct labour	2.25
General fixed overhead	1.00
	4.45

The fixed overhead is absorbed on the basis of direct labour hours. The components could be purchased for £3.65 each from the outside supplier.

Tasks

(i) Calculate the annual benefit of either purchasing or manufacturing the components, stating any assumptions.

(ii) Comment on another factor that the firm would need to consider before finalising a decision on whether to make or buy. (12 mins)

(d) The sales and profit figures of company A for two consecutive years are given below.

	Year 1	Year 2
Sales	£220,000	£280,000
Profit	£21,000	£36,000

(i) Calculate the sales necessary to earn a profit of £42,000.

(ii) Calculate the profit if sales were £188,000.   (12 mins)

3 JK COMPANY (25 mins)

You work as assistant accountant for the JK Company which manufactures four products. The results for the latest month, November, are as follows.

Profit statement for November

Product	J	K	L	M	Total
	£	£	£	£	£
Sales revenue	6,400	2,900	2,400	7,600	19,300
Variable costs	3,000	2,400	1,500	5,100	12,000
Contribution	3,400	500	900	2,500	7,300
Fixed costs	1,280	580	480	1,520	3,860
Profit	2,120	(80)	420	980	3,440

At a recent board meeting, the directors considered the continual poor performance of product K and now wish to evaluate the following proposal from the marketing director.

'Product K should be discontinued. I estimate that sales of the other three products would be affected as follows:

Product J	increase by 5%
Product L	decrease by 15%
Product M	increase by 25%

I have no idea what this will do to our monthly profitability but I do think that it is worth investigating.'

You have investigated the cost behaviour patterns and have found the following.

- None of the fixed costs are directly attributable to any of the products; they have been arbitrarily apportioned according to sales values.

- All variable costs vary in direct proportion to the product's sales value.

Tasks

(a) Prepare a profit statement which shows the effect on monthly profit of the marketing director's proposals.

State clearly any assumptions which you make.

(b) On the basis of your profit statement in Task 1 (a), state whether the marketing director's proposals should be accepted.

4 DELMAR (50 mins)

The Delmar company has produced the following information relating to the single product that it produces. For the coming year the firm plans to produce and sell 80,000 units.

	£
Direct wages	22
Direct materials	4
Variable overhead	2
Fixed overhead	4
Profit	8
Selling price	40

There is a possibility that unit wages costs will increase by 10% because of a new incentive scheme and this is not included in the above figures.

Tasks

(a) Draw a chart from which contribution and profit at levels of volume up to 80,000 units can be read. (15 mins)

(b) Prepare the adjustments necessary to show on the chart the effect of the possible cost increase outlined above. (8 mins)

(c) Show by calculation the profit expected in the following situations.

    (i) The current level of sales without the wages cost increase

    (ii) The current level of sales with the possible cost increase (5 mins)

(d) If there are no other cost changes, explain what volume of production and sales is required to maintain the current profit level if the wage increase occurs. (10 mins)

(e) Comment on the assumptions that are necessary to be made when preparing any form of breakeven chart. (12 mins)

5 CINEMA CHAIN (45 mins)

A cinema chain, based in Oxford, owns three cinemas in the towns of Newbury, Reading and Basingstoke. It has prepared budgets for the coming year based upon a ticket price of £4.

	Reading £	Newbury £	Basingstoke £	Total £
Budgeted ticket receipts	1,600,000	1,200,000	800,000	3,600,000
Costs				
Film hire	500,000	400,000	390,000	1,290,000
Wages and salaries	300,000	250,000	160,000	710,000
Overheads	500,000	400,000	350,000	1,250,000
	1,300,000	1,050,000	900,000	3,250,000

Included in the overhead figures are the Oxford head office fixed costs that amount to £720,000. These have been allocated to each cinema on the basis of budgeted ticket receipts. All other costs are variable.

The management are concerned about the Basingstoke cinema and the fact that it is showing a budgeted loss and is considering closing the cinema and selling the site to a property developer.

Tasks

(a) Prepare marginal costing statements to show contributions for each cinema and contribution and profit for the overall chain on the following bases.

    (i) The original budget

    (ii) If the Basingstoke cinema is closed (15 mins)

(b) State whether, on the grounds of profitability, you think that the Basingstoke cinema should be closed. Give a reasoned explanation of your decision. (6 mins)

(c) Calculate the contribution per ticket sale at each cinema. (8 mins)

(d) Calculate the margin of safety in revenue for the chain at the budgeted level of activity in the following circumstances.

    (i) If the Basingstoke cinema is kept open

    (ii) If the Basingstoke cinema is closed (8 mins)

(e) If the Basingstoke cinema is kept open management want an increase in profitability. One suggestion is that receipts at the cinema can be increased by 50% by an advertising campaign directed at Basingstoke that will add £40,000 to the chain's fixed costs.

Task

Explain whether the advertising campaign should be undertaken to improve the cinema's profitability. Give reasons for your decision. (8 mins)

6 SENSITIVE GAMES (25 mins)

Details of an indoor games centre are as follows.

Activity	Employees	Revenue £	Area Sq metres
Pool	5	30,000	2,200
Badminton	1	10,000	400
Indoor bowls	1	10,000	400
Snack bar	1	40,000	200
Administration	12	-	800

Costs	£
Cost of snack bar provisions	4,750
Cleaning materials for pool room	5,000
General costs	35,000

Employees are paid £5,000 per annum each.

General costs are to be apportioned to all activities on an area basis. Administration costs are to be re-apportioned to all other activities on the basis of employees.

Any surplus or deficit arising from the snack bar activities (after it has been charged with its appropriate allocations of cost) is to be allocated to the remaining activities on the basis of revenues.

Task

Prepare a statement showing the surplus or deficit for the pool, badminton and indoor bowls activities.

7 HOTEL (45 mins)

A large hotel has recently reorganised its costing system and split its activities into four cost centres as follows.

(a) Accommodation
(b) Catering
(c) Leisure
(d) Outings

The hotel is moving towards standardising its services and selling a hotel package to its customers which will include accommodation, meals, use of leisure facilities and a number of outings. There is to be a predetermined price per day for the use of each cost centre by the customer.

Labour and material can be identified and allocated to the cost centres in the budget but other overheads listed below cannot be so readily identified.

	Accommodation £	Catering £	Leisure £	Outings £	Total £
Labour	110,000	100,500	35,000	38,500	284,000
Materials	19,000	36,000	16,000	13,000	84,000
Power					84,000
Rent and rates					72,000
Depreciation					60,000
Advertising					76,000
Office expenses					240,000

You are given the following information about the cost centres from the budget for the coming year.

	Accommodation	Catering	Leisure	Outings
Floor area (in sq metres)	1,200	400	600	200
Number of employees	32	16	24	8
Machinery value	£10,000	£20,000	£60,000	£30,000
Kilowatt hours	5,000	2,500	12,500	1,000
Expected customer usage in days	15,000	12,000	8,000	3,000

You are told that advertising is to be apportioned to the cost centres on the basis of customer usage and office expenses apportioned on the basis of total cost per cost centre before the apportionment of the office expenses.

The budget for the coming year has been based upon the strategy that customers will have the standard accommodation and catering package with the leisure facilities and outings package as optional.

Hotel policy for the coming year is to operate a profit margin of 30% on price.

Tasks

(a) Prepare a cost statement for the four cost centres showing the budgeted total cost and the budgeted cost per customer day per cost centre. (15 mins)

(b) Calculate the price to be charged to a married couple who want to stay at the hotel for one week. They require accommodation and catering for seven days, use of the leisure facilities for three days and want to go on outings on three days. (10 mins)

(c) The actual results for the hotel for the year under review were as follows.

Cost centre	Total cost £	Customer usage Days
Accommodation	320,000	15,250
Catering	275,000	13,000
Leisure	200,000	6,800
Outings	125,000	3,200

Calculate the under/over absorption of costs per cost centre. (10 mins)

(d) The hotel manager is concerned about the costing policy used for food purchase. The materials for the catering cost centre are bought by the hotel's central staff and charged to the catering cost centre at standard cost as they are used. The standard is determined once a year and any variance is written off to the four cost centres on a monthly basis as part of the office expenses.

Food prices have been changing rapidly and purchases are continually being made at different prices as costs go up and down. The hotel manager now wants a system that charges food out to the catering cost centre on a basis that reflects the rapid movement of food prices.

Outline two alternative methods of pricing food stuffs to the catering cost centre and recommend to the hotel manager the one that meets his needs, clearly stating the reason for your choice.

(10 mins)

8 PRODUCT OMEGA (50 mins)

A firm manufactures and sells a single product called Product Omega.

Product Omega per unit

	£
Selling price	30
Direct costs	8

Details for the months of September and October are as follows:

	September	*October*
Production of Omega	750 units	1,000 units
Sales of Omega	600 units	1,150 units
Fixed production overheads	£4,500	£4,500

There was no opening stock at the beginning of September.

The normal level of activity for both sales and production is 900 units per month. Fixed production overheads are budgeted for £4,500 per month and are absorbed on a unit basis.

Tasks

(a) Why is it appropriate for a units basis for absorption to be used in this situation?

(5 mins)

(b) Prepare for September and October profit statements showing stock valuations, based on the principles of:

    (i) Absorption costing   (20 mins)

    (ii) Marginal costing   (15 mins)

(c) Reconcile the different profits calculated for absorption and marginal costing in (b).

(10 mins)

9 DELTA MANUFACTURING (50 mins)

The chairman of the Delta Manufacturing Company Limited faces a difficult board meeting. During December 20X2 the company lost £20,000 and the chairman's four colleagues on the board are far from happy. Each has put a pet proposal he would like to see adopted, at the expense, if need be, of his colleagues. The only thing that they do agree on is that a profit target of £40,000 per month is to be pursued.

To assist in evaluating each director's proposal, the chairman has invited you, as management accountant, to the meeting so that you may present the figure implied by the different proposals. You know that the company has a fixed cost of £200,000 per month and a variable cost per unit of £50 up to 12,000 units and £60 for units in excess of this figure. December 20X2 sales were 9,000 units.

The following independent proposals have been put forward.

(1) Improve the packaging of the product at a cost of £5 per unit and so increase sales

(2) Spend £20,000 on advertising per month

(3) Drop the selling price by £5 per unit

(4) Buy some more modern machinery which will cut variable costs by £10 per unit at all output levels (Sales would not alter.)

Task

Prepare a report for Delta's chairman on the proposals. The report should include statements which analyse the viability of each of the four proposals and evaluate each proposal in terms of what factors should be taken into consideration before that particular proposal is either accepted or rejected.

10 SMALL CONTRACTOR (50 mins)

A small contractor has been asked to quote for a contract which is larger than he would normally consider. The contractor would like to obtain the job as he does have surplus capacity.

The estimating and design department has spend 200 hours in preparing drawings and the following cost estimate.

Cost estimate	*Notes*	£	£
Direct materials:			
3,000 units of X at £10 (original cost)	(1)		30,000
100 units of Y (charged out using FIFO)			
50 units at £100		5,000	
50 units at £125		6,250	
			11,250
Direct materials to be bought in	(2)		12,000
Direct labour			
skilled staff	(4)		
2,720 hours at £5 per hour			13,600
trainees	(5)		
1,250 hours at £2 per hour			2,500
Depreciation on curing press	(6)		
Annual straight line depreciation (£12,000)			
Used for one month, depreciation charge			1,000
Subcontract work	(7)		20,000
Supervisory staff	(8)		6,150
Estimating and design department	(9)		
200 hours at £10 per hour		2,000	
Overtime premium for 50 hours		500	
			2,500
			99,000
Administration overhead at 5% of above costs	(10)		4,950
			103,950

Notes

(1) A sufficient stock of raw material X is held in the stores. It is the residue of a quantity bought some ten years ago. If this stock is not used on the prospective contract it is unlikely that it will be used in the foreseeable future. The net resale value is thought to be £20,000.

(2) Material Y is regularly used by the contractor on a variety of jobs. The current replacement cost of the material is £130 per unit.

(3) This is the estimated cost of the required material.

(4) Staff are hired on long-term contracts and are paid for a basic 40 hour week. The labour hour rate includes a charge of 100% of the wage rate to cover labour related overhead costs. It is estimated that, at the current level of operations, 80% of the overheads are variable. It is considered that one extra worker will be required temporarily for three months if the contract is obtained. His cost of £100 per week for

12 weeks (which includes the associated amount of 100% labour related overhead expense) is included in the estimate of £13,600.

(5) No additional trainees would be taken on. The trainees' wage rate is £1 per hour but their time is charged out at £2 to allow for labour related overhead on the same basis as in note 4 above.

(6) The curing press is normally fully occupied. If it is not being used by the contractor's own workforce it is being hired out at £500 per week.

(7) This is the estimated cost for the work.

(8) It is not considered that it would be necessary to employ any additional supervisory staff. The estimated cost of £6,150 includes an allowance of £1,000 for overtime which it may be necessary to pay to the supervisors.

(9) The expense of this department is predominantly fixed but the overtime payments were specifically incurred to get the drawings and plans out in time.

(10) The administrative expense is a fixed cost. This is the established method of allocating the cost to specific contracts.

It is considered that any quotation higher than £100,000 will be unsuccessful.

Tasks

(a) Prepare a revised cost estimate using an opportunity cost approach. State whether you consider that the revised calculation can provide support for a quotation below £100,000. (35 mins)

(b) Comment on the use of opportunity costs:

    (i)   for decision-making, and

    (ii)   for cost control purposes (15 mins)

11   MR BELLE (40 mins)

Mr Belle has recently developed a new improved video cassette and shown below is a summary of a report by a firm of management consultants on the sales potential and production costs of the new cassette.

Sales potential

The sales volume is difficult to predict and will vary with the price, but it is reasonable to assume that at a selling price of £10 per cassette, sales would be between 7,500 and 10,000 units per month. Alternatively, if the selling price was reduced to £9.00 per cassette, sales would be between 12,000 and 18,000 units per month.

Production costs

If production is maintained at or below 10,000 units per month, then variable manufacturing costs would be approximately £8.25 per cassette and fixed costs £12,125 per month. However, if production is planned to exceed 10,000 units per month, then variable costs would be reduced to £7.75 per cassette, but the fixed costs would increase to £16,125 per month.

Mr Belle has been charged £2,000 for the report by the management consultants and, in addition, he has incurred £3,000 development costs on the new cassette.

If Mr Belle decides to produce and sell the new cassette it will be necessary for him to use factory premises which he owns, but are leased to a colleague for a rental of £400 per month.

Also he will resign from his current post in an electronics firm where he is earning a salary of £1,000 per month.

Tasks

(a) Identify in the question an example of:

(i)   An opportunity cost

(ii) A sunk cost   (5 mins)

(b) Making whatever calculations you consider appropriate, analyse the report from the consultants and advise Mr Belle of the potential profitability of the alternatives shown in the report.

Any assumptions considered necessary or matters which may require further investigation or comment should be clearly stated.   (35 mins)

12   SHOE RETAILER (30 mins)

A shoe retailer prepares the following forecast for his shop for next year:

Pairs of shoes to be sold	24,000
Average selling price per pair	£40
Average cost per pair	£25
Staff costs for the year	£90,000
General office costs for the year	£150,000

Tasks

(a) Calculate the breakeven point in pairs of shoes to be sold, and the margin of safety.

(7 mins)

(b) Prepare a breakeven graph which indicates the breakeven point.   (12 mins)

(c) Give *three* advantages and *three* limitations of breakeven analysis.   (11 mins)

13   BREAKEVEN CHARTS (45 mins)

A friend of yours has come to you for financial advice. He is about to set up in business manufacturing and selling personal computers. He provides you with the following budgeted information concerning his total costs.

	£
Material costs	280,000
Labour costs	300,000
Production overhead	150,000
Selling and distribution overhead	140,000
Administration overhead	60,000

The above figures are based upon budgeted production of 3,500 computers, although there is production capacity for 4,000 computers. The budgeted selling price is £300 per computer.

You ascertain that £125,000 of labour costs, 100% of administration overheads, 30% of production overheads and 50% of selling and distribution overheads are fixed in nature. All other costs are variable with the level of production.

Tasks

(a) Prepare a cost statement showing the contribution per computer and for the budgeted level of production.   (14 mins)

(b) Calculate the profit at the budgeted level of production.   (3 mins)

(c) Construct a breakeven chart in good format, clearly showing the breakeven point in units and sales revenue as well as the margin of safety in units at the budgeted level of production. (14 mins)

(d) List and comment upon the major assumptions upon which breakeven charts are based. (7 mins)

(e) Your friend has had an offer to utilise his existing spare capacity by making 500 computers for a price of £225 per computer. He intends to reject this offer as the price is well below his total cost for making a computer. Advise him upon this course of action, giving reasons for your advice. (7 mins)

14   JETS LTD (41 mins)   AAT, 12/94

You work as the assistant management accountant for Jets Ltd, a company which specialises in warehousing and packing other companies' goods on a contract basis.

Your company has been approached by Sykes Ltd, who have offered Jets Ltd the contract to pack their product. Sykes will deliver the unpacked units and will collect the packed product on a regular basis. There will be no need to provide warehousing facilities.

You have carried out some preliminary costings and the results of your investigations are as follows.

Sykes contract

Estimated number of units to be packed each week =	200
Contract price per unit packed =	£27

Cost to be incurred at this activity level

Packing materials	£15.00 per unit packed
Packing labour	Salaries: £568 per week Bonuses: £0.80 per unit packed
Loading labour	Salaries: £350 per week Bonuses: £0.50 per unit loaded
Hire of packing machine	£100 per week
Administration and other costs	£480 per week

Assume that all units packed are loaded in the same week.

The costs staged above relate solely to this contract. For example, the labour will be employed full-time on this contract work.

Tasks

(a) Prepare a cost and profit statement for one week of this contract, which shows the following.

   (i)   Variable costs in total and per unit
   (ii) Fixed costs in total and per unit
   (iii) Profit in total and per unit (17 mins)

(b) Calculate the following for the contract.

   (i)   The breakeven point in units per week
   (ii) The margin of safety for an activity level of 200 units per week
   (iii) The profit which would be earned if activity is increased by 20% to 240 units (12 mins)

(c) Prepare a memorandum to the managing director which contains the following.

   (i)   Brief comments on the forecast results for this contract

    (ii)   An explanation of the problems involved in using the data supplied to forecast the profit result for an activity level of 240 units per week   (12 mins)

15   SECURITY SERVICES (30 mins)   AAT, 6/94

The company for which you work provides security services for corporate clients. It currently charges £30 per hour for the service and the cost structure of the service is as follows.

Variable cost per hour	£22
Fixed cost for one month	£18,000

The marketing director has suggested that the company should provide extra benefits to its services. Research conducted amongst current customers suggests that they would be prepared to pay £33 per hour for the improved service. The cost structure would be altered as follows.

Revised variable cost per hour	£20
Revised fixed cost for one month	£39,000

It is not expected that sales levels would alter from the current level of 5,200 hours per month.

Tasks

(a)   Calculate the breakeven point in hours per month both in the present situation and with the changes proposed by the marketing director.   (8 mins)

(b)   Calculate the monthly profit both in the present situation and with the changes proposed by the marketing director.   (12 mins)

(c)   Comment briefly on the way that the revised cost and selling price structure will affect future profit changes if sales increase or decrease from their current level.

    (10 mins)

16   SINGLE PRODUCT (75 mins)   AAT, 4/94

The following information relates to a month's production of ABC Ltd, a small manufacturing company mass-producing a single product.

	ABC Ltd
Materials	£4.00
Labour cost per unit	£6.00
Fixed costs per month	£40,000
Production capacity per month	10,000 units
Selling price per unit	£17.00
Current level of sales per month	7,000 units

(a)   *Task*

    Using graph paper, prepare a breakeven chart for the company. Show clearly the breakeven point and the position for current level of sales per month.   (21 mins)

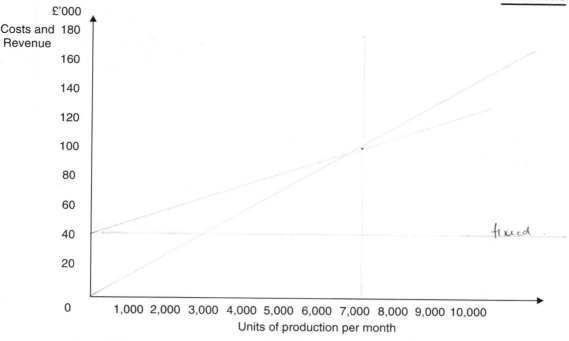

Note. For the purposes of this specimen question, only an outline of the graph's axes has been produced. Graph paper will be provided, if needed, in the 'live' assessments.

(b) *Tasks*

    (i)   Calculate the breakeven point in units using the formula rather than reading off from the graph.   (9 mins)

    (ii)   Calculate the current level of profit per month.   (9 mins)

(c) DEF Ltd is a competitor with the same production capacity as ABC Ltd and selling a similar product at the same price. DEF Ltd has fixed costs of £60,000 per month and variable costs of £5.00 per unit.

    Task

    (i)   Contrast the production methods of ABC Ltd and DEF Ltd from the information given.   (9 mins)

    (ii)   Which of the two companies will generate profits at a higher rate for levels of production beyond its breakeven point? Give reasons for your answer.

    (9 mins)

(d) The marketing manager of ABC Ltd suggests that the company should increase the product's selling price to £20 and upgrade the quality of the product by spending an additional £2.00 per unit on materials. Fixed costs would be increased by £2,000. It is estimated that sales per month would drop to 6,500 units.

    Task

    What would be the effect on ABC Ltd's profitability of implementing the above policy?

    (18 mins)

17   BUILDING COMPANY (50 mins)

A building company constructs a standard unit which sells for £30,000. The company's costs can be readily identifiable between fixed and variable costs.

Budgeted data for the coming six months includes the following.

	Sales Units	Profit £
January	18	70,000
February	20	100,000
March	30	250,000
April	22	130,000
May	24	160,000
June	16	40,000

You are told that the fixed costs for the six months have been spread evenly over the period under review to arrive at the monthly profit projections.

Tasks

(a) Prepare a graph for total sales, costs and output for the six months under review that shows the following.

    (i)   The breakeven point in units and revenue
    (ii)   Total fixed costs
    (iii) The variable cost line
    (iv) The margin of safety for the total budgeted sales   (25 mins)

(b) The company is worried about the low level of sales. The sales director says that if the selling price of the unit was reduced by £5,000 the company would be able to sell 10% more units. All other costs would remain as above.

    Determine whether the company should reduce the selling price to attract new sales in order to maximise profit. Show clearly any workings.   (10 mins)

(c) Evaluate whether the assumption that costs are readily identifiable as either fixed or variable throughout a range of production is realistic. Give examples of any alternative classification.   (15 mins)

18 ELECTRICITY (45 mins)

A business is considering whether to supply a store with goods on a one-year contract to the value of £70,000, although the costings established for the contract suggest that a loss would result.

Contract costing

	£
Material for the goods	
Material C	14,000
Material F	7,000
Operating labour	30,000
Supervisory labour	12,000
Depreciation of machinery	10,000
General overheads	21,000
Total cost	94,000
Revenue	70,000
Loss	(24,000)

The following information is established.

(a) Material C is already in stock, having been purchased some time ago at a cost of £14,000. It cannot be used for any other purpose, and if not used on this contract would have to be disposed of at a cost to the business of £2,000.

(b) Material F was bought for £7,000 last year. It could be used on existing orders as a substitute for Material X which is not in stock and which would cost £9,000 to buy.

(c) Operating labour would consist of three workers who would be transferred from other departments in the business. These workers earn £200 per week each. Their place in the other departments would be taken by three new employees working on a one year contract who would each be paid £220, including necessary overtime. Assume 50 weeks per year.

(d) The cost of supervisory labour (£12,000) is an allocation of part of the salary of a supervisor who is in overall charge of several production lines.

(e) The machinery which would be used to produce the toys was purchased nine years ago at a cost of £100,000, with an estimated life of ten years. The depreciation charge in the costing represents the charge for the final year of the machinery's life. The machinery has been idle for some time, and if not used on this order the machinery would be scrapped for a revenue of £2,000. After use on this contract the machinery would have no value, and would have to be disposed of at a cost estimated at £1,500.

(f) General overheads represent an allocation to the contract of part of the firm's total overheads, based on an absorption rate of 100% of material costs. There are no specific general overheads which the contract would incur.

Task

Give your recommendations whether on financial grounds the contract should be undertaken.

Your calculations must be supported by clear statements of the reasons why a particular figure is included or excluded, and of any assumptions that you make. (30 mins)

19 CONSULTANCY (15 mins)

An information technology consultancy firm has been asked to do an urgent job by a client, for which a price of £2,500 has been offered. The job would require the following.

(a) 30 hours' work from one member of staff, who is paid on an hourly basis, at a rate of £20 per hour, but who would normally be employed on work for clients where the charge-out rate is £45 per hour. No other member of staff is able to do the member of staff in question's work.

(b) The use of 5 hours of mainframe computer time, which the firm normally charges out to external users at a rate of £50 per hour. Mainframe computer time is currently used 24 hours a day, 7 days a week.

(c) Supplies and incidental expenses of £200.

Should the firm accept the job?

20 KATRINA (40 mins)

Katrina Limited is considering launching a new project, code named 'The Wave'. Market research was carried out costing £10,000, which indicated that each of the new products could easily be sold at £50 per unit. To commence the manufacture it is necessary however to buy an item of capital equipment costing £150,000. The machine will last the length of the project, which is thought to be five years. The machine will have no residual value in year five. Variable costs are 25% of the selling price and specific fixed costs £50,000. Sales demand is expected to be constant throughout the life of the project at 5,000 units per year. No capital allowances are available on the capital expenditure.

Task

(a) Calculate the NPV of the Wave project using a cost of capital of 10%. (10 mins)

(b) Calculate the percentage by which each of the following must change for the NPV to become zero (ie its 'sensitivity').

    (1)   Variable costs
    (2)   Capital outlay
    (3)   Volume of sales
    (4)   Fixed costs   (20 mins)

(c) Discuss any limitations in the technique applied or any assumptions made in parts (a) and (b).   (10 mins)

21   STAPLES LTD (15 mins)

The mean weekly take-home pay of the employees of Staples Ltd and a price index for the 11 years from 20X0 to 20Y0 are as follows.

Year	Weekly wage £	Price index (20X0 = 100)
20X0	150	100
20X1	161	103
20X2	168	106
20X3	179	108
20X4	185	109
20X5	191	112
20X6	197	114
20X7	203	116
20X8	207	118
20X9	213	121
20Y0	231	123

Construct a time series of real wages for 20X0 to 20Y0 using a price index with 20X6 as the base year.

22   INFLATION INDEX (5 mins)

Given a cash flow of £X in n year's time (year n) and an inflation index of a in the current year and b in year n, how would you calculate the value of £X today?

23   SEASONAL VARIATIONS (20 mins)

A statistician is carrying out an analysis of a company's production output. The output varies according to the season of the year and from the data she has calculated the following seasonal variations, in units of production.

	Spring	Summer	Autumn	Winter
Year 1			+ 11.2	+ 23.5
Year 2	− 9.8	− 28.1	+ 12.5	+ 23.7
Year 3	− 7.4	− 26.3	+ 11.7	

Required

Calculate the average seasonal variation for each season.

24 PROJECT APPRAISAL CALCULATIONS I

A company is considering investing in a project for which the following information is provided.

			£
Initial capital expenditure			75,000
Profits/(losses):	year 1		40,000
	year 2		30,000
	year 3		10,000
	year 4		(10,000)
	year 5		(10,000)

Notes

(a) The project will be operational for five years, at the end of which time there is not expected to be any scrap value. Depreciation is provided on a straight line basis.

(b) The company estimates its cost of capital at 15% and discount factors are as follows.

Year 1	0.870
Year 2	0.756
Year 3	0.658
Year 4	0.572
Year 5	0.497

Tasks

Calculate the following.

(a) The payback period in years
(b) The net present value
(c) The accounting rate of return based on average investment

Guidance notes

1   This question will give you some basic practice of three commonly used appraisal techniques. Remember the following rules.

2   Cash flows are used in payback and net present value calculations. If you are given accounting profits (as in this question) you must add back the depreciation charge in order to convert the figures from profits to cash flows.

3   Accounting profits are used in calculating the accounting rate of return. Accounting profits are taken after depreciation.

25 PROJECT APPRAISAL CALCULATIONS II

The management of a laundry is considering whether to purchase a new piece of equipment which would cost £200,000.

40,000 items are expected to be laundered in each of the five years of the equipment's life.

The revenue from each item laundered is expected to be £4, and budgeted operating costs are £2 per item.

General fixed overheads will be assigned to the equipment each year as follows:

Depreciation - £40,000

General fixed overheads - £80,000, based on 100% of operating costs.

Tasks

(a) Calculate the payback period for the equipment.
(b) Calculate the net present value for the equipment.

Note. The management expect that the cost of capital will remain constant at 20% pa.

BPP PUBLISHING

	Discount factor
Year 1	0.833
Year 2	0.694
Year 3	0.579
Year 4	0.482
Year 5	0.402

(c) If the number of units to be laundered each year was to be increased by 10%, calculate the percentage increase in net present value.

Guidance notes

1   It is necessary to make an assumption about the general fixed overhead. Words such as 'assigned', 'general' and 'allocated' usually indicate that the overheads would be incurred anyway and so are not relevant.

2   Remember to state your assumptions.

26   FOUR PROJECTS (45 mins)

A company has called upon you for advice. It has a capital investment budget for the year of £300,000 and there are four projects in which they are keen to invest over the coming year. However they can only invest in one project. They intend using the proceeds of a 12% debenture (loan) issue to fund the project investment. If any of the funds are not used they can be invested at 12%.

The company has no system for investment appraisal and called in a management consultant for guidance and received the following information from him.

Project	Cost of project £	Payback period	Accounting rate of return	Net present value £	Internal rate of return
A	300,000	1.5 years	30%	190,000	17%
B	300,000	2.0 years	40%	270,000	23%
C	300,000	3.0 years	50%	240,000	21%
D	300,000	2.5 years	20%	(10,000)	11%

Unfortunately the management consultant did not explain the above.

Tasks

(a) Explain to the company the mechanics of each investment appraisal method and how it is applied.   (15 mins)

(b) After your explanation the sales director says the company should invest in project A as costs are recovered the quickest. The production director says that the company should invest in project C as it gives the best results in terms of return. The personnel director says that the company should invest in project B as that gives the highest discounted present value and internal rate of return. The managing director wants you to resolve the problem.

Advise the managing director as to which proposal you agree with, outlining the reasons for your decision and the reasons why you have rejected the other two proposals.   (10 mins)

(c) The board of the company are unclear why you are using the 12% rate associated with the debentures in your calculations for two of the methods outlined in (a) above. They maintain that the raising of finance has nothing to do with the investment of that finance.

Set out the reasons as to why the 12% figure has been used in your calculations in (a) above and identify which investment appraisal methods have used it.   (10 mins)

(d) It is conceivable that the risk attached to the projects will increase before the investment is undertaken. In these circumstances the main objective of the company would be to keep the risk in the project investment to a minimum.

Outline how this will change your answer to (b) above, if at all, giving explanations for your decision. (5 mins)

(e) The circumstances might arise that the company has funds to invest in all projects.

Present a reasoned analysis as to whether investment in all projects should be undertaken. (5 mins)

27 LOAMSHIRE LIBRARY (22 mins) AAT, 4/94

The information given below relates to the library service operated by the Leisure Services Committee of Loamshire County Council.

In order to reduce operating expenses over the next four or five years, there is a proposal to introduce a major upgrade to the computer system used by the library service. Two alternative projects are under examination with different initial outlays and different estimated savings over time. The computer manager has prepared the following schedule.

	Project A £	Project B £
Initial outlay	75,000	100,000
Annual cash savings:		
1st year	20,000	30,000
2nd year	30,000	45,000
3rd year	30,000	45,000
4th year	25,000	40,000
5th year	20,000	-

Assume that the cash savings occur at the end of the year, even though in practice they would be spread over the year. From a technical point of view, both systems meet the librarian's specification. It is assumed that there will be no further savings after year 5 and it may be necessary to install a new system by that date. The county uses the net present value method at a 10% discount rate for evaluating projects (see the table below).

Task

Prepare a report to the County Librarian giving your recommendations. Include the relevant calculations in your report. She is not familiar with DCF calculations and has asked you to explain why the authority uses a DCF technique in preference to the 'payback' method of appraising capital projects.

Present value of £1.00 at a discount rate of 10%

Number of years from the present	£
1	0.9091
2	0.8264
3	0.7513
4	0.6830
5	0.6209
6	0.5645

28 WASH ME (45 mins) AAT, 6/94

A transport company is considering purchasing an automatic vehicle cleansing machine. At present all vehicles are cleaned by hand.

The machine will cost £80,000 to purchase and install and it will have a useful life of four years with no residual value.

The operating costs of the machine will amount to £8,000 in the first year, increasing by 5% each year in line with the number of vehicles cleaned. Savings in labour costs will be £25,000 each year.

In addition to using the machine for its own vehicles, the company will be able to clean vehicles for other organisations. Revenue from this service will amount to £14,000 each year. Additional direct costs of 10% of revenue will be incurred for every vehicle cleaned on behalf of another organisation.

The company uses a discount rate of 10% to appraise all capital projects.

Task

As Assistant Management Accountant, you are asked to carry out an appraisal of the proposal to purchase the machine and to prepare a report to the general manager of the company. Your report should contain the following information.

(a) The net present value of the cash flows from the project.
(b) The payback period of the proposal.
(c) A recommendation as to whether the proposal should be accepted.

In your calculations you should ignore the effects of inflation and assume that all cash flows occur at the end of the year.

Note. The present value of £1 at a discount rate of 10% is as follows.

Number of years from the present	£
1	0.9091
2	0.8264
3	0.7513
4	0.6830

29 INVESTMENT PROJECTS (45 mins)

A company is trying to decide which of two investment projects it should choose. The following information is provided.

	Project 1	*Project 2*
	£	£
Capital expenditure	75,000	75,000
Profit - Year 1	30,000	25,000
Profit - Year 2	30,000	15,000
Profit - Year 3	20,000	20,000
Profit (or loss) - Year 4	(10,000)	20,000
(Loss) - Year 5	(10,000)	(15,000)

Notes

(1) Each project is expected to be operational for 5 years, at the end of which time there is not expected to be any scrap value.

(2) Capital expenditure for both projects would be incurred immediately.

(3) The profit figures are shown after including depreciation on a straight line basis.

(4) Taxation is to be ignored.

(5) The company's cost of capital is 15%.

(6) The present value of £1 received in pounds at the end of:

Year 1:   0.869
Year 2:   0.756
Year 3:   0.657
Year 4:   0.571
Year 5:   0.497
Year 6:   0.432

Tasks

(a) Calculate for each project:

  (i) The payback period in years to 1 decimal place
  (ii) The net present value   (25 mins)

(b) State the relative merits of the methods of evaluation mentioned in (a) above.

                                                                                                       (12 mins)

(c) Explain which project you would recommend for acceptance.   (8 mins)

30   PRODUCT Q (45 mins)

A company is proposing to enter a new market and has collected the following data.

Capital expenditure on plant and machinery to produce Product Q will total £1,500,000 to be paid immediately. During the first year while the plant is being erected and machinery installed no production or sales of Product Q is expected.

Sales of Product Q are expected to be 12,500 units each year from Year 2 to Year 5 inclusive. At the end of Year 5 the plant and machinery will be sold for scrap with cash receipts estimated at £100,000.

Data per unit of Product Q:

	£
Selling price	80
Variable cost	(30)
Fixed overheads	(30)
Profit	20

Cost and revenue data are expected to remain constant throughout the project's lifetime.

The fixed overhead of £30 per unit is made up of depreciation (£28) and general overhead (£2). The general overheads are the company's fixed costs which are allocated to each product on the basis of an absorption rate of 6.66% of unit variable cost. There are no fixed costs which are specific to this project.

The company's cost of capital is 20% pa.

Year	Discount factor
1	0.833
2	0.694
3	0.579
4	0.482
5	0.402

Tasks

(a) Calculate:

  (i) The average accounting rate of return on average capital employed to *one* decimal place

  (ii) The net present value   (25 mins)

(b) Discuss the relative merits of the accounting rate of return and net present value methods of investment appraisal, and explain whether you would undertake the project.   (20 mins)

31   TRANSPORT FLEET (50 mins)

Your company is considering investing in its own transport fleet. The present position is that carriage is contracted to an outside organisation. The life of the transport fleet would be five years, after which time the vehicles would have to be disposed of.

The cost to your company of using the outside organisation for its carriage needs is £250,000 for this year. This cost, it is projected, will rise 10% per annum over the life of the project. The initial cost of the transport fleet would be £750,000 and it is estimated that the following costs would be incurred over the next five years.

	Drivers' costs £	Repairs & maintenance £	Other costs £
Year 1	33,000	8,000	130,000
Year 2	35,000	13,000	135,000
Year 3	36,000	15,000	140,000
Year 4	38,000	16,000	136,000
Year 5	40,000	18,000	142,000

Other costs include depreciation. It is projected that the fleet would be sold for £150,000 at the end of year 5. It has been agreed to depreciate the fleet on a straight line basis.

To raise funds for the project your company is proposing to raise a long-term loan at 12% interest rate per annum.

You are told that there is an alternative project that could be invested in using the funds raised which has the following projected results.

> Payback = 3 years
> Accounting rate of return = 30%
> Net present value = £140,000

As funds are limited, investment can only be made in one project.

Note. The transport fleet would be purchased at the beginning of the project and all other expenditure would be incurred at the end of each relevant year.

Tasks

(a) Prepare a table showing the net cash savings to be made by the firm over the life of the transport fleet project. (10 mins)

(b) Calculate the following for the transport fleet project.

  (i) Payback period
  (ii) Accounting rate of return
  (iii) Net present value

The discount factors for 12% are as follows.

Year	
1	0.893
2	0.797
3	0.712
4	0.636
5	0.567

(20 mins)

(c) Write a short report to the investment manager in your company outlining whether investment should be committed to the transport fleet or the alternative project outlined. Clearly state the reasons for your decision. (20 mins)

32 GT COMPANY (45 mins)

The GT Company estimates that it can save £2,800 in cash costs for each of the next ten years if it invests now in a new machine that has just become available for £11,000. There is no expected scrap value and the company uses a rate of 14% as a desired return.

Tasks

(a) Calculate the following.

(i)   The payback period
(ii) The net present value

The following discount factors at 14% apply.

Year	
1	0.8772
2	0.7695
3	0.6750
4	0.5921
5	0.5194
6	0.4556
7	0.3996
8	0.3506
9	0.3075
10	0.2697

(10 mins)

(b) (i)   Explain if the firm should invest in this new machine, based on your calculations.

(ii) Explain what other factors a firm would need to consider, other than financial ones, when making a decision like the one illustrated.   (10 mins)

(c) The GT Company is also considering introducing an incentive scheme to remunerate its employees. At present each employee receives £42 for an eight hour day, and on average each employee produces 15 units of good output a day.

Production overhead costs are all fixed and are absorbed into unit costs at £4 per labour hour.

Under the proposed system each unit of good output will be paid for as follows.

Units of good output per day	Remuneration per unit
16	£2.92
17	£2.98
18	£3.04
19	£3.10
20	£3.16

Task

Prepare a report detailing economic advantages or disadvantages to the firm of adopting this scheme.   (25 mins)

33 PROJECTS T AND R (45 mins)

(a) *Task*

Explain why net present value is considered technically superior to payback and accounting rate of return as an investment appraisal technique even though the latter are said to be easier to understand by management. Highlight the strengths of the net present value method and the weaknesses of the other two methods.

(12 mins)

(b) Your company has the option to invest in projects T and R but finance is only available to invest in one of them.

You are given the following projected data.

	Project	
	T	R
	£	£
Initial cost	70,000	60,000
Profits: Year 1	15,000	20,000
Year 2	18,000	25,000
Year 3	20,000	(50,000)
Year 4	32,000	10,000
Year 5	18,000	3,000
Year 6		2,000

You are told the following.

(i) All cash flows take place at the end of the year apart from the original investment in the project which takes place at the beginning of the project.

(ii) Project T machinery is to be disposed of at the end of year 5 with a scrap value of £10,000.

(iii) Project R machinery is to be disposed of at the end of year 3 with a nil scrap value and replaced with new project machinery that will cost £75,000.

(iv) The cost of this additional machinery has been deducted in arriving at the profit projections for R for year 3. It is projected that it will last for three years and have a nil scrap value.

(v) The company's policy is to depreciate its assets on a straight line basis.

(vi) The discount rate to be used by the company is 14% and appropriate discount factors are as follows.

Year	
1	0.877
2	0.769
3	0.675
4	0.592
5	0.519
6	0.465

Tasks

(i) If investment was to be made in project R, determine whether the machinery should be replaced at the end of year 3.

(ii) Calculate the following for projects T and R, taking into consideration your decision in (i) above.

(1) Payback period
(2) Net present value

Advise which project should be invested in, stating your reasons. (25 mins)

(c) *Task*

Explain what the discount rate of 14% represents and state two ways of how it might have been arrived at. (8 mins)

34 HOTEL GROUP (45 mins)

The management of a hotel group is deciding whether to scrap an old but still serviceable machine bought five years ago to produce fruit pies, and replace it with a newer type of machine.

It is expected that the demand for the fruit pies will last for a further five years only and will be as follows.

	Produced and sold number of pies
Year 1	40,000
Year 2	40,000
Year 3	30,000
Year 4	20,000
Year 5	20,000

The fruit pies are currently sold for £3 per pie.

Each machine is capable of meeting these requirements.

Data for the two machines is as follows.

	Existing machine £	New machine £
Capital cost	320,000	150,000
	£ per unit	£ per unit
Operating costs:		
Direct labour	0.60	0.40
Materials	0.60	0.60
Variable overheads	0.30	0.25
Fixed overheads:		
Depreciation	0.80	1.00
Allocated costs (100% direct labour costs)	0.60	0.40
	2.90	2.65

Unit operating costs, fixed overhead costs and selling price are expected to remain constant throughout the five year period.

Tasks

(a) Using data relating only to the new machine:

    (i)   Calculate the payback period of the new machine

    (ii)   Calculate the net present value of the new machine

Note. The hotel group expects that its cost of capital will be 20% pa throughout the period. (20 mins)

(b) Assume that the existing machinery could be sold for £130,000 immediately, if it was replaced. Show, using present value calculations, whether the existing machine should be replaced by the new machine.

Year	Discount factor at 20%
1	0.833
2	0.694
3	0.579
4	0.482
5	0.402

(15 mins)

(c) Assume that no new machinery can be purchased, but that an outside caterer has offered to supply all of the hotel group's requirements for fruit pies at a price which compares favourably with the group's own cost of producing the pies. What factors other than price would need to be considered before making a decision whether to accept the offer? (10 mins)

35 PRINTING (38 mins) AAT, 12/94

Your organisation currently uses a specialist printing company to provide all of its requirements for headed stationery, annual reports, publicity material and so on.

Consideration is now being given to setting up an in-house printing facility and cancelling the contract with the printing company. A single penalty payment of £4,000 would be charged but the annual saving would be £33,000 which is paid to the printing company under the terms of the contract.

Machines costing £12,400 will be purchased. They will last for four years and will have no value at the end of this time. The operating costs of the new printing department will amount to £27,200 each year. This includes staff salaries, material costs, hire of equipment, administration and so on.

In addition to using the facility for your organisation's own purposes, it will be possible to undertake printing jobs for other organisations, earning incremental revenue of £1,600 each year. Incremental direct costs of this service will amount to 30% of revenue.

Tasks

(a) Calculate the net present value of the cash flows from the proposal, using a 12% discount rate over four years.

Ignore the effects of taxation and inflation and assume that all cash flows occur at the end of the year.

Note. The present value of £1 at a discounted rate of 12% is as follows.

Number of years from the present	£
1	0.89
2	0.80
3	0.71
4	0.64

(21 mins)

(b) Calculate the payback period for the proposal and explain the advantages and disadvantages of the use of this appraisal method. (17 mins)

36 FUTURISTIC LTD (20 mins)

Futuristic Ltd is considering whether or not to invest in a new labour-saving item of equipment. Forecasts of costs and savings from the equipment are as follows, at today's prices:

Equipment cost: £105,000

Savings in labour costs

	£
Year 1	20,000
Year 2	30,000
Years 3 - 5	25,000 per annum

Savings in materials costs

	£
Year 1	4,000
Year 2	6,000
Year 3 - 5	5,000 per annum

Estimated residual value of equipment, beginning of year 6 £20,000

The expected rates of inflation in costs for the next six years are as follows.

Labour costs	10% per annum
Materials costs	5% per annum
Equipment costs	3% per annum

The company's money cost of capital is 20%.

Tasks

(a) What is the NPV of the project?
(b) What is the IRR of the project (use 20% and 25% discount rates for your calculation)?
(c) Should the project be undertaken?

37 CONTRACT LTD (30 mins)

Contract Ltd has been offered a contract which, if accepted, will begin on 1 January 20X7. It will last for three years. The price offered is £45,600 of which £12,000 is payable on 31 December 20X7, £12,000 on 31 December 20X8 and £21,600 on 31 December 20X9.

Four items of cost are relevant to the contract:

(1) *Materials.* Only one type of material, material X, will be used on the contract, 1,000 units will be required in all, 500 as soon as the contract is commenced and 500 at the end of 20X7. At present, 500 units of material X, which cost £18 per unit in 20X6 are in stock. The material is in regular use and stocks are replaced as they are used. Payment for replacement stock is made when the order is placed. The current buying price (at 1 January 20X7) is £18.60 per unit, and this is expected to increase by 5% by 31 December 20X7.

(2) *Labour.* Three unskilled workers will each spend three years on the contract. Their current wage rate is £30 per week each. In addition, a sub-contractor will be required to spend thirteen weeks on the contract in 20X7 and thirteen weeks in 20X9. At present, he is paid £40 per week. The firms intends to give a 10% wage increase to all employees and sub-contractors on 1 January 20X8 and a further 10% increase on 1 January 20X9.

(3) *Machinery.* The machinery required for the contract will be leased by the firm at an annual rental of £2,400 payable in arrears and fixed for three years. The machinery will be required for the full three years of the contract.

(4) *Overhead expenses.* Overhead expenses are normally recovered at a rate of 50% on labour costs. The level of total overhead expenses will be unaffected by undertaking the contract.

Assume that none of the firm's resources is in short supply and that all cash flows (excluding the purchase of the first 500 units of material X) arise on the last day of the year in which they fall due.

The general price level index presently stands at 100, and is expected to increase at the rate of 7% per annum compound for the indefinite future. Contract Ltd has a cost of capital, in 'money' terms of 11%.

Tasks

(a) Prepare calculations showing whether acceptance of the contract is worthwhile; and

(20 mins)

(b) Justify the method you use for appraising the contract; deal particularly with your treatment of inflation. (10 mins)

Note. Ignore taxation.

Practice devolved assessments

PRACTICE DEVOLVED ASSESSMENT 1

RANE LTD   **AAT, 6/95**

Time allowed – 2 hours plus 15 minutes reading time.

You are advised to spend approximately 45 minutes on Section 1, 40 minutes on Section 2 and 35 minutes on Section 3.

SECTION 1

Data

You work as a trainee for a small management consultancy which has been asked to advise a company, Rane Limited, which manufactures and sells a single product. Rane is currently operating at full capacity, producing and selling 25,000 units of their product each year. The cost and selling price structure for this level of activity is as follows.

	At 25,000 units output	
	£ per unit	£ per unit
Production costs		
Direct material	14	
Direct labour	13	
Variable production overhead	4	
Fixed production overhead	8	
Total production cost		39
Selling and distribution overhead		
Sales commission - 10% of sales value	6	
Fixed	3	
		9
Administration overhead		
Fixed		2
Total cost		50
Mark-up (20%)		10
Selling price		60

A new managing director has recently joined the company and he has engaged your organisation to advise on his company's selling price policy. The sales price of £60 has been derived as above from a cost plus pricing policy. The price was viewed as satisfactory because the resulting demand enabled full capacity operation.

You have been asked to investigate the effect on costs and profit of an increase in the selling price. The marketing department has provided you with the following estimates of sales volumes which could be achieved at the three alternative sales prices under consideration.

Selling price per unit	£70	£80	£90
Annual sales volume (units)	20,000	16,000	11,000

You have spent some time estimating the effect that changes in output volume will have on cost behaviour patterns and you have now collected the following information.

Direct material

The loss of bulk discounts means that the direct material cost per unit will increase by 15% for all units produced in the year if activity reduces below 15,000 units per annum.

Direct labour

Savings in bonus payments will reduce labour costs by 10% for all units produced in the year if activity reduces below 20,000 units per annum.

Sales commission

This would continue to be paid at the rate of 10% of sales price.

Fixed production overhead

If annual output volume was below 20,000 units then a machine rental cost of £10,000 per annum could be saved. This will be the only change in the total expenditure on fixed production overhead.

Fixed selling overhead

A reduction in the part-time sales force would result in a £5,000 per annum saving if annual sales volume falls below 24,000 units. This will be the only change in the total expenditure on fixed selling and distribution overhead.

Variable production overhead

There would be no change in the unit cost for variable production overhead.

Administration overhead

The total expenditure on administration overhead would remain unaltered with this range of activity.

Stocks

Rane's product is highly perishable; therefore no stocks are held.

Task 1

(a) Calculate the annual profit which is earned with the current selling price of £60 per unit.

(b) Prepare a schedule to show the annual profit which would be earned with each of the three alternative selling prices.

Task 2

Prepare a brief memorandum to your boss, Chris Jones. The memorandum should cover the following points.

(a) Your recommendation as to the selling price which should be charged to maximise Rane Limited's annual profits.

(b) *Two* non-financial factors which the management of Rane Limited should consider before planning to operate below full capacity.

SECTION 2

Data

Another of your consultancy's clients is a manufacturing company, Shortage Limited, which is experiencing problems in obtaining supplies of a major component. The component is used in all of its four products and there is a labour dispute at the supplier's factory which is restricting the component's availability.

Supplies will be restricted to 22,400 components for the next period and the company wishes to ensure that the best use is made of the available components. This is the only component used in the four products and there are no alternatives and no other suppliers.

The components cost £2 each and are used in varying amounts in each of the four products.

Shortage Limited's fixed costs amount to £8,000 per period. No stocks are held of finished goods or work in progress.

The following information is available concerning the products.

	Product A	*Product B*	*Product C*	*Product D*
Maximum demand per period	4,000 units	2,500 units	3,600 units	2,750 units
	£ per unit	£ per unit	£ per unit	£ per unit
Selling price	14	12	16	17
Component costs	4	2	6	8
Other variable costs	7	9	6	4

Task

(a) Prepare a recommended production schedule for next period which will maximise Shortage Limited's profit.

(b) Calculate the profit that will be earned in the next period if your recommended production schedule is followed.

SECTION 3

Data

You are employed as the assistant accountant in your company and you are currently working on an appraisal of a project to purchase a new machine. The machine will cost £55,000 and will have a useful life of three years. You have already estimated the cash flows from the project and their taxation effect and the results of your estimates can be summarised as follows.

Year	1	2	3
Post-tax cash inflow	£18,000	£29,000	£31,000

Your company uses a post-tax cost of capital of 8% to appraise all projects of this type.

Task 1

(a) **Calculate the net present value of the proposal to purchase the machine.**

   Ignore the effects of inflation and assume that all cash flows occur at the end of the year.

   Note: the present value of £1 at a discount rate of 8% is as follows.

Number of years from the present	£
1	0.93
2	0.86
3	0.79

(b) **Calculate the payback period for the investment in the machine.**

Task 2

The marketing director has asked you to let her know as soon as you have completed your appraisal of the project. She has asked you to provide her with some explanation of your calculations and of how taxation affects the proposal.

Prepare a memorandum to the marketing director which answers her queries. Your memorandum should contain the following.

(a) **Your recommendation concerning the proposal.**

(b) **An explanation of the meaning of the net present value and the payback period**

(c) **An explanation of the effects of taxation on the cash flows arising from capital expenditure.**

PRACTICE DEVOLVED ASSESSMENT 2

NORTH AND SOUTH

Time allowed – 2 hours plus 15 minutes reading time.

You are advised to spend approximately 50 minutes on Section 1, 40 minutes on Section 2 and 30 minutes on Section 3.

SECTION 1

Data

You are employed by Green and Co, a firm of accountants based in Anytown. One of your clients, Mr Smith, is considering purchasing an existing milk delivery round. This involves purchasing milk in standard sized bottles from a dairy and delivering them to householders each morning.

The current owner of the delivery round is hesitant to disclose too much financial information until preliminary contracts have been signed. Your client, however, has been given two audited statements. These show the turnover and profit for the last two months are as follows.

Month	*October*	*November*
Turnover	£34,720	£33,600
Operating profit	£4,180	£3,900

The only fixed costs relate to the rental of a small warehouse from the dairy, which is used to garage the vehicle and store the deliveries of milk, plus an all-inclusive leasing charge for the delivery vehicle. The vehicle is also owned by the dairy. A colleague had confirmed with the dairy that these fixed costs total £4,500 per month. In addition, the dairy disclosed that there had been no change in the cost of milk sold to owners of delivery rounds during October and November. Your client believes these are the only costs other than the cost of buying the milk from the dairy and that there has been no change in the price of milk sold to customers for at least four months.

Task 1

Prepare a statement for Mr Smith:

(a)   **identifying turnover, the cost of milk sold, the contribution and the profit for each month;**

(b)   **estimating for each month the breakeven sales turnover and the percentage fall in turnover possible before a loss is made.**

Data

It is now two weeks later and you have received a letter from Mr Smith. In the letter, the following queries are raised.

(a)   I do not understand the term 'contribution'. What does this mean?

(b)   The current owner has been selling milk for 40p per bottle over the last six months. How many bottles need to be sold to break even each month and how many were sold in November?

(c)   I believe I need to make a profit of £1,500 per month to compensate for giving up my current job. How many bottles of milk will I need to sell each month to achieve this?

(d)   Supermarkets are currently selling milk for much less than 40p per pint. To compete, I believe I will have to reduce my price to 38p. How many bottles will I have to sell to break even, how many will I have to sell to make a profit of £1,500 per month and what are the wider implications of selling at the reduced price?

Task 2

Write a letter to Mr Smith answering the individual points raised above.

SECTION 2

Data

It is currently December 20X5. You are an assistant management accountant with North and South. The company makes several products, two of which are the Handy and the Super. The unit selling price and costs for both are reproduced below. All are current costs.

Handy	£	*Super*	£
Selling price	100	Selling price	102
Material X - 2 litres	32	Material Y - 3 kilograms	30
Labour - grade 1	24	Labour - grade 2	32
Overheads based on labour hours	24	Overheads based on labour hours	32
Unit profit	20	Unit profit	8

The contracts director of North and South, Elizabeth Brookes, is considering whether to bid for a contract. Already the development department has spent 150 person-hours on preliminary work and this amount will double if a full bid is made. The charge-out rate for the development department is £250 per hour of which £50 relates to general overheads. However, the overhead component will double in the immediate future to allow for the department only working at 50 per cent capacity. In addition to these costs, the contract will require three types of material.

The contract calls for 1,000 kilograms of material A. North and South currently have 1,500 kilograms in stock although the company has no further use for it. It originally cost £10 per kilogram but was subsequently written down to £8 per kilogram. The current purchase price is £9 while any surplus stock can be sold for £7 per kilogram.

Material B is also no longer used in the company. The contract requires 1,500 litres of which 600 litres is in stock. Originally this cost £20 per litre although the current purchase price is £24. If not used in the contract, Material B could either be sold to a competitor for £14 per litre or used as a replacement for material X in the making of the Handy. For each litre of Material B used, North and South could save purchasing one litre of material X.

Material C is used regularly by North and South and 2,000 kilograms will be required by the contract. North and South operates a first-in-first-out stock valuation system and the current stocks are 500 units at a unit cost of £7 purchased on 20 October 20X5 and 700 units costing £7.50 per unit purchased on 8 November 20X5. Additional supplies are available at a unit price of £8 and any surplus stocks can be sold for £7.50 each.

The contract calls for 2,000 hours of labour grade 2, the rate for which is £16 per hour. This includes a 100 per cent overhead recovery rate. Currently there is a severe shortage of this quality of labour. If the contract is won, North and South will have to take employees away from producing the Super.

The contract will also require the use of two machines for six months. These are special, heavy-duty machines although they will only be required for light work on the contract. The depreciation charge per annum using the straight-line method is £20,000 per machine. For the first three months of the contract, they would have no further use but for the second three months, North and South has entered into an arrangement to rent them to another company for a total of £18,000. Less sophisticated machines suitable for use on the contract are available for hire at £2,000 per machine per month.

North and South have a company-wide policy to add 100 per cent to all contract costs to cover general overheads.

Task 1

Elizabeth Brookes has asked for your advice about the contract. She is particularly concerned to estimate the minimum bid price which would not involve a loss for North and South.

Prepare a statement recommending the minimum price at which it would be viable for North and South to undertake the contract.

Task 2

Write a short memo to Elizabeth Brookes:

(a)   Explaining and justifying by way of example the accounting technique or techniques you have used in deriving the minimum bid price

(b)   Justifying why you believe the individual costs of each resource associated with the contract should be included in your statement in answer to Task 1

SECTION 3

Data

RBG plc is a large quoted company with a 25 per cent cost of capital for appraising capital projects. One of its divisional directors has put forward plans to make a new product, the A1. This will involve buying a machine specifically for that task. The machine will cost £600,000 and have a life of 5 years. However, because of the nature of the product, the machine will have no residual value at any time. All sales will be for cash, no stocks will exist at the year-end and purchases and labour will be paid currently. The overheads relate to the rent of premises specifically acquired to produce the A1.

The divisional director has put forward the following details in support of the proposal.

	£
Turnover per annum	380,000
Material	90,000
Labour	30,000
Overheads	20,000
Straight line depreciation per annum	120,000
Annual profit	120,000

The divisional accountant has recommended that the proposal should be rejected as £120,000 only represents a 20 per cent return on the capital cost of the proposal.

Task

You are asked to write a report to the divisional accountant:

(a) Explaining the limitations to the approach taken in the initial project appraisal

(b) Reappraising the divisional director's proposal, using the net present value method of evaluating discounted cash flows, and interpreting the result

(c) Calculating the discounted payback period and explaining its possible use

Notes

Taxation and inflation can be ignored and, for the calculation of the net present value, it can be assumed that cash flows occur at the end of each year.

The present value of £1 at a discount rate of 25 per cent is as follows.

End of year	£	End of year	£
1	0.800	4	0.410
2	0.640	5	0.328
3	0.512	6	0.262

PRACTICE DEVOLVED ASSESSMENT 3

QUALITY DATA PRODUCTS   AAT, 6/96

Time allowed – 2 hours plus 15 minutes reading time.

You are advised to spend approximately 50 minutes on Section 1, 35 minutes on Section 2 and 35 minutes on Section 3.

SECTION 1

Data

You have recently been appointed as the Management Accountant to Quality Data Products Ltd. QDP was started almost five years ago by Peter Dixon to manufacture an improved television aerial. For the first four years, the company could sell as many units as it could make. Because of this, it was agreed to charge overheads to production based on the company's maximum manufacturing capacity.

However, Hilary Farmer, the company's Finance Director, believes that the likely level of sales and production for the full twelve months of the current year will fall to 2.4 million units. On this assumptions, she has prepared a forecast statement of profitability for year five.

Forecast income statement 12 months ended 30 June 20X6

	£	£
Turnover		120,000,000
Variable material	26,160,000	
Variable labour	34,080,000	
Variable production overhead	10,560,000	
Fixed production overhead absorbed*	19,200,000	
		90,000,000
Gross profit		30,000,000
Sales commission**	6,000,000	
Fixed selling expenses	11,500,000	
Fixed administration expenses	5,000,000	
Unabsorbed fixed production overhead*	4,800,000	
		27,300,000
Operating profit		2,700,000

* Total fixed production overhead comprises fixed overhead absorbed and charged to production plus fixed overhead unabsorbed and charged as an expense of the year
** Based on sales turnover

Hilary explained that the reason for the reduced profit was partly due to reduced sales volume arising from a competitor entering the market and partly due to QDP no longer being able to claim a 20% discount on material costs because production had fallen below 2.5 million aerials.

Peter Dixon put forward three proposals to improve profitability next year. The first was to reduce prices by 8%, the second to reduce prices by 12%. If prices were reduced by 8%, he felt demand would increase to 2.8 million aerials per year but if prices fell by 12% the demand was likely to be 3.5 million aerials. The third proposal was to manufacture an improved product.

This third proposal would involve a £12 million marketing campaign to launch the revised aerial. In addition, a new material would have to be used. This would cost 10% more than the current material and the supplier would not offer any quantity discounts. However, because of the improved quality of the material, the variable labour cost per aerial would fall by £2.00 and there would be no other changes. If the new product was launched, Peter believes volume would return to the level of the previous four years.

Task 1

On the assumption that sales and production volumes equal one another, you are asked to prepare a statement identifying the likely profitability of Quality Data Products next year for each of the three proposals.

Data

On receiving your statement, Hilary Farmer informs you that Peter Dixon was not absolutely certain that the volumes suggested for the three proposals would be achieved. She also mentioned that he had not considered any of the wider, non-financial implications of the proposals.

Task 2

Hilary Farmer asks you to prepare a memorandum. The memorandum should:

(a) Estimate the volume of sales necessary for each of the three proposals where profitability would be the same as in the current year

(b) Identify two non-financial matters which should be considered before making a final decision

SECTION 2

Data

Chemical Compounds Ltd comprises three divisions. The Exta division uses a single raw material, X1, to make chemicals Y1 and Z1. Because of the nature of the process, it is impossible to make one chemical without the other. The only uses for the chemical are as raw materials in products made by Chemical Compounds' other two divisions. Exta invoices these divisions at cost plus 20 per cent for any Y1 or Z1 used.

The second of Chemical Compounds' divisions, the Yetum division, uses chemical Y1 as a raw material in Yetum production. There is a regular and increasing demand for Yetum from a variety of customers. However, if there was surplus production, it would cost £70 to destroy an unused litre of Y1.

The third division, the Zorba division, uses chemical Z1 in the production of Zorba. National Chemicals plc is the only possible customer for Zorba production. National Chemical plc have entered into a long-term contract to purchase 150,000 litres of Zorba each year but have said that they are unlikely to require more than this amount in the foreseeable future. No other use exists for the Zorba and any surplus Z1 would have to be destroyed at a cost of £40 per litre.

Each year, the Exta division uses 200,000 litres of raw material X1. There is no wastage or other loss and, after adding labour and overheads, production is 50,000 litres of Y1 and 150,000 litres of Z1 - a proportion determined by the process. These inputs are than converted to 50,000 litres of Yetum and 150,000 litres of Zorba as a result of adding labour and overheads. All three processes use a common grade of labour which costs £30 per hour. Apportioned general overheads are charged out on the basis of labour hours.

The results for the year to 31 May 20X6 are reproduced below. The cost of plant overhead is unique to each division and would be saved if the division was closed down.

Chemical Compounds Ltd divisional profitability year to 31 May 20X6

	Exta Division £	Yetum Division £	Zorba Division £
Material	40,000,000	17,400,000	52,200,000
Labour	6,000,000	3,000,000	6,000,000
Plant overhead	8,000,000	6,000,000	4,000,000
Apportioned general overhead	4,000,000	2,000,000	4,000,000
Total expenses	58,000,000	28,400,000	66,200,000
Revenue	69,600,000	20,000,000	90,000,000
Profit/(loss)	11,600,000	(8,400,000)	23,800,000

At a board meeting to consider the results, anxiety is expressed about the performance of the Yetum division. Two options are being considered: one is to close down the Yetum division, the other is to increase Yetum production in order to spread the overheads over a greater output while maintaining its market price.

Task 1

You have been asked by the Financial Director of Chemical Compounds Ltd to carry out a financial evaluation of the proposals currently being considered by the board. You should prepare two statements:

(a) A statement showing the effect on annual profit if the Yetum division is closed down

(b) A statement of the unit profitability of any *additional* Yetum sales and production

Data

After preparing your statements, you are informed that there has been a change of policy at National Chemical plc. As a result of increased demand for their products, they are interested in purchasing an extra 30,000 litres of Zorba each year. However, they argue that Chemical Compounds Ltd are already recovering all their overheads in the current contract price. Because of this, National Chemicals would only be prepared to pay half the current price per litre for the extra purchases.

Task 2

Prepare a report for the Financial Director. Your report should:

(a) **Evaluate the effect of National Chemicals' proposal on the profitability of Chemical Compounds Ltd**

(b) **Identify two other factors which should be considered by the Board before a final decision is made**

Note. Task 2 should be considered independently of your solution to Task 1.

SECTION 3

Data

You are employed by Brown and Co, a firm of accountants in Anytown. One day, you are visiting Henry Evans, a client. Henry owns Metal Parts Ltd, a small factory manufacturing car accessories. The business has proven a great success but he is now operating close to full capacity. Because of this, he is considering buying an additional machine costing £120,000. If he acquires a new machine, he will have to lease additional premises next to his existing factory at a yearly cost of £10,000.

Cashflow is not a particular problem for Henry. He carries no stocks, pays his suppliers at the time of purchase and normally receives payment immediately a sale is made.

Henry has prepared some preliminary information for you. The new machine will last for four years and will have no residual value. It will qualify for a 25% annual writing down allowance based on the reducing balance and any outstanding capital allowances at the end of the machine's life can be claimed as a balancing allowance in the final year. The only problem is that Metal Parts Ltd has to pay corporation tax at 30% on taxable profits. Henry shows you his workings. (These are reproduced below.)

Year	Turnover £	Material £	Labour £	Rent £	Depreciation £	Pre-tax profit £	After tax profit £
1	100,000	40,000	20,000	10,000	30,000	0	0
2	120,000	48,000	20,000	10,000	30,000	12,000	8,400
3	140,000	56,000	20,000	10,000	30,000	24,000	16,800
4	160,000	64,000	20,000	10,000	30,000	36,000	25,200
							50,400

Henry feels he should go ahead and purchase the machine. 'Deducting 30% from the pre-tax profits, my total after tax profits will be £50,400', he explains. 'Last time you were here, you told me that my required return was 10%. On that basis, buying the machine is extremely profitable.'

Task

Prepare a report to Henry Evans. Your report should:

(a) Use the net present value technique to identify whether or not the planned acquisition of the machine is worthwhile

(b) Explain to Henry your approach to taxation in investment appraisal

Notes

Inflation can be ignored. For the purpose of this task, you may assume the machine would be purchased at the beginning of the accounting year and that there is a one-year delay in paying corporation tax. All cashflows - other than the purchase of the machine - can be assumed to occur at the end of each year. Henry has no other assets on which he can claim capital allowances.

The present value of £1 at a discount rate of 10 per cent is as follows.

End of year	Discount factor
1	0.909
2	0.826
3	0.751
4	0.683
5	0.621
6	0.564

PRACTICE DEVOLVED ASSESSMENT 4

YORK PLC   **AAT, 12/96**

Time allowed – 2 hours plus 15 minutes reading time.

You are advised to spend approximately 55 minutes on Section 1 and 65 minutes on Section 2.

SECTION 1

Data

York plc was formed three years ago by a group of research scientists to market a new medicine that they had invented. The technology involved in the medicine's manufacture is both complex and expensive. Because of this, the company is faced with a high level of fixed costs.

This is of particular concern to Dr Harper, the company's chief executive. She recently arranged a conference of all management staff to discuss company profitability. Dr Harper showed the managers how average unit cost fell as production volume increased and explained that this was due to the company's heavy fixed cost base. 'It is clear,' she said, 'that, as we produce closer to the plant's maximum capacity of 70,000 packs, the average cost per pack falls. Producing and selling as close to that limit as possible must be good for company profitability.' The data she used is reproduced below.

Production volume (packs)	40,000	50,000	60,000	70,000
Average cost per unit*	£430	£388	£360	£340

Current sales and production volume: 65,000 packs. Selling price per pack: £420.

*Defined as the total of fixed and variable costs divided by the production volume.

You are a member of York plc's management accounting team and shortly after the conference you are called to a meeting with Ben Cooper, the company's marketing director. He is interested in knowing how profitability changes with production.

Task 1

Ben Cooper asks you to calculate:

(a)   The amount of York plc's fixed costs
(b)   The profit of the company at its current sales volume of 65,000 packs
(c)   The break-even point in units
(d)   The margin of safety expressed as a percentage

Data

Ben Cooper now tells you of a discussion he has recently had with Dr Harper. Dr Harper had once more emphasised the need to produce as close as possible to the maximum capacity of 70,000 packs. Ben cooper has the possibility of obtaining an export order for an extra 5,000 packs but, because the competition is strong, the selling price would only be £330. Dr Harper has suggested that this order should be rejected as it is below cost and so will reduce company profitability. However, she would be prepared, on this occasion, to sell the packs on a cost basis for £340 each, provided the order was increased to 15,000 packs.

Task 2

Write a memo to Ben Cooper. Your memo should:

(a) Calculate the change in profits from accepting the order for 5,000 packs at £330

(b) Calculate the change in profits from accepting an order for 15,000 packs at £340

(c) Briefly explain and justify which proposal, if either, should be accepted

(d) Identify *two* non-financial factors which should be taken into account before making a final decision

SECTION 2

Data

The Portsmere Hospital operates its own laundry. Last year, the laundry processed 120,000 kilograms of washing and this year the total is forecast to grow to 132,000 kilograms. This growth in laundry processed is forecast to continue at the same percentage rate for the next seven years. Because of this, the hospital must immediately replace its existing laundry equipment. Currently, it is considering two options, the purchase of machine A or the rental of machine B. Information on both options is given below.

Machine A - purchase		*Machine B - rent*	
Annual capacity (kilograms)	180,000	Annual capacity (kilograms)	170,000
Material cost per kilogram	£2.00	Material cost per kilogram	£1.80
Labour cost per kilogram	£3.00	Labour cost per kilogram	£3.40
Fixed costs per annum	£20,000	Fixed costs per annum	£18,000
Life of machine	3 years	Rental per annum	£20,000
Capital cost	£60,000	Rental agreement	3 years
Depreciation per annum	£20,000	Depreciation	nil

The hospital is able to call on an outside laundry if there is either a breakdown or any other reason why the washing cannot be undertaken in-house. The charge would be £10 per kilogram of washing. Machine A, if purchased, would have to be paid for immediately. All other cashflows can be assumed to occur at the end of each year.

Machine A will have no residual value at any time. The existing laundry equipment could be sold for £10,000 cash. The fixed costs are a direct cost of operating the laundry. The hospital's discount rate for projects of this nature is 15%.

Task

You are an accounting technician employed by the Portsmere Hospital and you are asked to write a brief report to its chief executive. Your report should:

(a) **Evaluate the two options for operating the laundry, using discounted cashflow techniques**

(b) **Recommend the preferred option and identify *one* possible non-financial benefit**

(c) **Justify your treatment of the £10,000 cash flow of the existing equipment**

(d) **Explain what is meant by discounted cashflow**

Notes

Inflation can be ignored. An extract from the present value tables used by the hospital is reproduced below.

End of year	*Discount factors*		
	10%	15%	20%
1	0.909	0.870	0.833
2	0.826	0.756	0.694
3	0.751	0.658	0.579
4	0.683	0.572	0.482
5	0.621	0.497	0.402
6	0.564	0.432	0.335
7	0.513	0.376	0.279

PRACTICE DEVOLVED ASSESSMENT 5

BRITA BEDS LTD   AAT, 6/97

Time allowed – 2 hours plus 15 minutes reading time.

You are advised to spend approximately 70 minutes on Section 1 and 50 minutes on Section 2.

SECTION 1

Data

You are employed as an accounting technician by Smith, Williams and Jones, a small firm of accountants and registered auditors. One of your clients is Winter plc, a large department store. Judith Howarth, the purchasing director for Winter plc, has gained considerable knowledge about bedding and soft furnishings and is considering acquiring her own business.

She has recently written to you requesting a meeting to discuss the possible purchase of Brita Beds Ltd. Brita Beds has one outlet in Mytown, a small town 100 miles from where Judith works. Enclosed with her letter was Brita Beds' latest profit and loss account. This is reproduced below.

BRITA BEDS LTD
PROFIT AND LOSS ACCOUNT - YEAR TO 31 MAY 20X7

Sales	Units	£
Model A	1,620	336,960
Model B	2,160	758,160
Model C	1,620	1,010,880
Turnover		2,106,000

Expenses	£	
Cost of beds	1,620,000	
Commission	210,600	
Transport	216,000	
Rates and insurance	8,450	
Light, heat and power	10,000	
Assistants' salaries	40,000	
Manager's salary	40,000	
		2,145,050
Loss for year		39,050

Also included in the letter was the following information.

(a)   Brita Beds sells three types of bed, models A to C inclusive.

(b)   Selling price are determined by adding 30% to the cost of beds.

(c)   Sales assistants receive a commission of 10% of the selling price for each bed sold.

(d)   The beds are delivered in consignments of 10 beds at a cost of £400 per delivery. This expense is shown as *Transport* in the profit and loss account.

(e)   All other expenses are annual amounts.

(f)   The mix of models sold is likely to remain constant irrespective of overall sales volume.

Task 1

In preparation for your meeting with Judith Howarth, you are asked to calculate:

(a)   The minimum number of beds to be sold if Brita Beds is to avoid making a loss
(b)   The minimum turnover required if Brita Beds is to avoid making a loss

51

Data

At the meeting, Judith Howarth provides you with further information, as follows.

(a)   The purchase price of the business is £300,000.

(b)   Judith has savings of £300,000 currently earning 5% interest per annum which she can use to acquire Brita Beds.

(c)   Her current salary is £36,550.

To reduce costs, Judith suggests that she should take over the role of manager as the current one is about to retire. However, she does not want to take a reduction in income. Judith also tells you that she has been carrying out some marketing research. The results of this are as follows.

(a)   The number of households in Mytown is currently 44,880.

(b)   Brita Beds Ltd is the only outlet selling beds in Mytown.

(c)   According to a recent survey, 10% of households change their beds every 9 years, 60% every 10 years and 30% every 11 years.

(d)   The survey also suggested that there is an average of 2.1 beds per household.

Task 2

Write a letter to Judith Howarth. Your letter should:

(a)   **Identify the profit required to compensate for the loss of salary and interest**

(b)   **Show the number of beds to be sold to achieve that profit**

(c)   **Calculate the likely maximum number of beds that Brita Beds would sell in a year**

(d)   **Use your answers in (a) to (c) to justify whether or not Judith Howarth should purchase the company and become its manager**

(e)   **Give *two* possible reasons why our estimate of the maximum annual sales volume may prove inaccurate**

Data

On receiving your letter, Judith Howarth decides she would prefer to remain as the purchasing director for Winter plc rather than acquire Brita Beds Ltd. Shortly afterwards, you receive a telephone call from her. Judith explains that Winter plc is redeveloping its premises and that she is concerned about the appropriate sales policy for Winter's bed department while the redevelopment takes place. Although she has a statement of unit profitability, this had been prepared before the start of the redevelopment and has assumed that there would be in excess of 800 square metres of storage space available to the bed department. Storage space is critical as customers demand immediate delivery and are not prepared to wait until new stock arrives.

The next day, Judith Howarth sent you a letter containing a copy of the original statement of profitability. This is reproduced below.

Model	A	B	C
Monthly demand (beds)	35	45	20
	£	£	£
Unit selling price	240.00	448.00	672.00
Unit cost per bed	130.00	310.00	550.00
Carriage inwards	20.00	20.00	20.00
Staff costs	21.60	40.32	60.48
Departmental fixed overheads	20.00	20.00	20.00
General fixed overheads	25.20	25.20	25.20
Unit profit	23.20	32.48	(3.68)
Storage required per bed (square metres)	3	4	5

In her letter, she asks for your help in preparing a marketing plan which will maximise the profitability of Winter's bed department while the redevelopment takes place. To help you, she has provided you with the following additional information.

(a) Currently storage space available totals 300 square metres.

(b) Staff costs represent the salaries of the sales staff in the bed department. Their total cost of £3,780 per month is apportioned to units on the basis of planned turnover.

(c) Departmental fixed overhead of £2,000 per month is directly attributable to the department and is apportioned on the number of beds planned to be sold.

(d) General fixed overheads of £2,520 are also apportioned on the number of beds planned to be sold. The directors of Winter plc believe this to be a fair apportionment of the store's central fixed overheads.

(e) The cost of carriage inwards and the cost of beds vary directly with the number of beds purchased.

Task 3

(a) **Prepare a recommended monthly sales schedule in units which will maximise the profitability of Winter plc's bed department.**

(b) **Calculate the profit that will be reported per month if your recommendation is implemented.**

SECTION 2

Data

Sound Equipment Ltd was formed five years ago to manufacture parts for hi-fi equipment. Most of its customers were individuals wanting to assemble their own systems. Recently, however, the company has embarked on a policy of expansion and has been approached by JBZ plc, a multinational manufacturer of consumer electronics. JBZ has offered Sound Equipment Ltd a contract to build an amplifier for its latest consumer product. If accepted, the contract will increase Sound Equipment's turnover by 20%.

JBZ's offer is a fixed price contract over three years although it is possible for Sound Equipment to apply for subsequent contracts. The contract will involve Sound Equipment purchasing a specialist machine for £150,000. Although the machine has a 10 year life, it would be written off over the three years of the initial contact as it can only be used in the manufacture of the amplifier for JBZ.

The production director of Sound Equipment has already prepared a financial appraisal of the proposal. This is reproduced below. With a capital cost of £150,000 and total profits of £60,300, the production director has calculated the return on capital employed as 40.2%. As this is greater than Sound Equipment's cost of capital of 18%, the production director is recommending that the board accepts the contract.

Proposal to build amplifier for JBZ plc

	Year 1 £	Year 2 £	Year 3 £	Total £
Turnover	180,000	180,000	180,000	540,000
Materials	60,000	60,000	60,000	180,000
Labour	40,000	40,000	40,000	120,000
Depreciation	50,000	50,000	50,000	150,000
Pre-tax profit	30,000	30,000	30,000	90,000
Corporation tax at 33%	9,900	9,900	9,900	29,700
After-tax profit	20,100	20,100	20,100	60,300

You are employed as the assistant accountant to Sound Equipment Ltd and report to John Green, the financial director, who asks you to carry out a full financial appraisal of the proposed contract. He feels that the production director's presentation is inappropriate. He provides you with the following additional information.

(a)   Sound Equipment pays corporation tax at the rate of 30%.

(b)   The machine will qualify for a 25% writing down allowance on the reducing balance.

(c)   The machine will have no further use other than in manufacturing the amplifier for JBZ.

(d)   On ending the contract with JBZ, any outstanding capital allowances can be claimed as a balancing allowance.

(e)   The company's cost of capital is 18%.

(f)   The cost of materials and labour is forecast to increase by 5% per annum for years 2 and 3.

John Green reminds you that Sound Equipment operates a Just in Time stock policy and that production will be delivered immediately to JBZ who will, under the terms of the contract, immediately pay for the deliveries. He also reminds you that suppliers are paid immediately on receipt of goods and that employees are also paid immediately.

Task

Write a report to the financial director. Your report should:

(a)   Use the net present value technique to identify whether or not the initial three year contract is worthwhile

(b)   Explain your approach to taxation in your appraisal

(c)   Identify *one* other factor to be considered before making a final decision

Notes

For the purpose of this task, you may assume the following.

(a)   The machine would be purchased at the beginning of the accounting year.
(b)   There is a one year delay in paying corporation tax.
(c)   All cashflows - other than the purchase of the machine - occur at the end of each year.
(d)   Sound Equipment has no other assets on which to claim capital allowances.

An extract from the present value tables used by Sound Equipment Ltd is reproduced below.

End of year	16%	17%	18%	19%	20%
1	0.862	0.855	0.847	0.840	0.833
2	0.743	0.731	0.718	0.706	0.694
3	0.641	0.624	0.609	0.593	0.579
4	0.552	0.534	0.516	0.499	0.482
5	0.476	0.456	0.437	0.419	0.402
6	0.410	0.390	0.370	0.352	0.335
7	0.354	0.333	0.314	0.296	0.279

PRACTICE DEVOLVED ASSESSMENT 6

FORTUNE PLC   **AAT, 12/97**

Time allowed – 2 hours plus 15 minutes reading time.

You are advised to spend approximately 75 minutes on Section 1 and 45 minutes on Section 2.

SECTION 1

Data

Fortune plc has three divisions. One of these is the Taste division, which manufactures a flavouring ingredient used in the food industry. The ingredient is produced using a 24-hour continuous process. Because of this, total output cannot exceed 100,000 litres per year. Currently, this is not a problem as the Taste division is operating below capacity.

You are employed as the assistant management accountant in Fortune's head office. In seven days' time, the directors are meeting to consider the budgets for the forthcoming year. Reproduced below is the budgeted operating statement for the Taste division.

Taste Division

Budgeted Operating Statement for the year to 31 December 20X8

	£'000	£'000
Turnover		16,000
Variable material	6,400	
Variable labour	3,200	
Variable overhead	1,600	
Fixed production overhead absorbed *	640	
		11,840
Gross profit		4,160
Sales commission (5% of turnover)	800	
Fixed selling expenses	600	
Fixed administration expenses	400	
Fixed production overhead unabsorbed *	160	
		1,960
Operating profit		2,200

*Fixed production overhead rates are based on maximum capacity

---

Task 1

In preparation for the meeting, you have been asked to provide the directors with additional information. (In providing this information, you should assume no change in unit selling price, no change in unit variable costs and no change in the cost of fixed expenses.) The directors ask you to calculate the following.

(a)   **Taste Division's budgeted sales volume in litres for the year to 31 December 20X8**

(b)   **Taste Division's break-even point in litres and value**

(c) **The percentage decrease in budgeted sales which will result in the division breaking even**

Data

Another division of Fortune plc is the Colouring Division. This division produces food colourings and also uses a 24-hour continuous process. Its maximum capacity - which cannot be exceeded - is 120,000 litres per year. The divisional management accountant gives you the working papers for the Colouring Division and a copy of this is shown below.

Working papers for the 20X8 budget - Colouring Division	
Maximum capacity of division (litres)	120,000
Planned sales to existing customers (litres)	100,000
Marginal cost per litre	£60
Contribution per litre	£40
Divisional fixed costs	£2,400,000

He tells you that the Colouring Division has not been able to prepare its budget for 19X8 as its sales manager is still considering a large special order from a new customer. He also gives you the following information:

- The special order is for a minimum of 30,000 litres.

- The agreed price will be £90 per litre.

- The Colouring Division is able to obtain an identical product to its own from a competitor in another country at a cost of £105 per litre inclusive of import duties and transport to the Colouring Division's premises.

Task 2

Write a brief memo to the sales manager of the Colouring Division. Your memo should:

(a) **Identify the budgeted turnover and profitability of the Colouring Division if the special order is *not* accepted**

(b) **Show the change in budgeted profit of accepting the special order of 30,000 litres if:**

    (i)   The division is not allowed to purchase any of the product from the competitor

    (ii) The division is allowed to purchase from the competitor

(e) **Identify *two* non-financial issues to be considered before making a final decision on the special order**

Data

Fortune's third division is the Packaging Division. This division blends ingredients. These are then sold to customers who then resell them to the public using their own brand names. The sales manager of the Packaging Division is considering accepting a contract and has asked for your advice. The customer has offered to pay £85,000 for the completed contract, but this is less than the estimated cost prepared by the sales manager. The estimate is reproduced below.

Proposed Contract - Estimated Costs

Expenditure	Quantity	Cost
Material A	1,000 kilograms	£30,000
Material B	2,000 kilograms	£40,000
Labour	1,000 hours	£8,000
Divisional fixed overheads	1,000 hours	£8,000
		£86,000

A colleague of yours in the Packaging Division provides you with the following additional information.

- Material A is regularly used in the division. Its standard cost is £30 per kilogram, although the current purchase price is £28 per kilogram.

- Material B is no longer used in the business, although 500 kilograms are still in stock at its original cost of £20 per kiogram. This stock could be sold for £13,000. Its current purchase price is £28 per kilogram.

- There is a single class of labour throughout the division. Each production employee is paid a flat rate of £280 per 35-hour week, although for costing purposes this is converted to an hourly rate.

- Divisional fixed overheads are 100% of the labour rate.

- Employees working in excess of 35 hours are paid an overtime rate of £10 per hour.

- The division has a policy of no redundancies, although over the life of the contract there will be 900 spare labour hours because of a shortage of orders.

Task 3

Prepare notes for the sales manager. Your notes should:

(a) Recommend the minimum contract price which would avoid the Packaging Division making a loss

(b) *Briefly* explain the technique or techniques you have used to calculate the minimum contract price

(c) Explain how you used the technique or techniques to obtain the cost of the labour and the divisional fixed overheads

SECTION 2

Data

You are an accounting technician employed in the management accounting department of Brendon Engineering Ltd and Ann Spring is the company's marketing director. Last week, she was offered a contract by a major customer. After discussing the details of the contract with Brendon Engineering's production director and the company's financial controller, she has turned to you for further advice. The contract would be for four years and Brendon Engineering would have to purchase a special machine costing £100,000. Although production would be 10,000 units in the first year, this would grow by 10% per year in each of the following three years. At the end of the fourth year, the machine would have no further use and its residual value would be negligible. Ann Spring's working papers are shown below.

Working papers	
Units to be produced and sold in the first year of the contract	10,000
Annual growth in sales volume and production	10%
Selling price per unit	£42
Material cost per unit	£20
Labour cost per year for production up to 12,000 units	£150,000
Labour cost per unit in excess of 12,000	£20
Annual rent of premises for each of the four years	£20,000
Apportionment of central overheads to contract	£1,000
Annual depreciation of machine purchased for the contract	£25,000

Ann Spring also provides you with the following information.

- A clause in the contract specifies that the customer must pay for units immediately on delivery.

- Brendon Engineering pays suppliers on receipt of materials.

- The company plans to carry no stocks for this contract.

- Employees' wages are paid in the period in which they are incurred.

- Brendon Engineering's cost of capital is 30%.

- If the contract is accepted, Brendon Engineering will have to rent premises as it is currently working at full capacity.

- All cashflows - other than the initial outlay - can be assumed to occur at the end of each year.

Task

Ann Spring has asked you to prepare a report on the proposed contract. Your report should:

(a) **Calculate the net present value of the proposed contract using Brendon Engineering's 30% cost of capital**

(b) **Calculate the net present value of the proposed contract using a discount rate of 70%**

(c) Use the solutions to parts (a) and (b) to determine the internal rate of return for the contract

(d) Explain what is meant by the internal rate of return

Notes

Inflation and risk can be ignored. An extract from the discounted cash flow tables used by Brendon Engineering Ltd is reproduced below.

End of year	Discount factors	
	30%	70%
1	0.769	0.588
2	0.592	0.346
3	0.455	0.204
4	0.350	0.120
5	0.269	0.070

Trial run
devolved
assessments

TRIAL RUN DEVOLVED ASSESSMENT 1

ALLBRIGHT METALS

Coverage of performance criteria

	Element 16.1: Prepare cost estimates	Tasks
1	The extent of the information to be contained within estimates is agreed with those who commission them	1,2,3
2	Appropriate staff are consulted about technical aspects and any special features of work activity and projects which impact upon costs	1,2,3
3	Current material, labour and other variable costs are identified and future trends assessed	1,2,3,4
4	Estimates account for the effect of possible variations in capacity on fixed overhead rates	2
5	Estimates are prepared in an approved form and presented to the appropriate people within an agreed timescale	1,2,3,4
	Element 16.2: Recommend ways to improve cost ratios and revenue generation	
1	Information relevant to estimating current and future costs and revenue is identified and used as the basis of analysis	1,2,3
2	Critical factors which may affect costs and revenue are analysed using appropriate accounting techniques and clear conclusions are drawn from the analysis	2,3
3	The views of appropriate specialists are gathered and used to inform analysis and any conclusions drawn	1,2,3
4	The assumptions made and the degree of accuracy which exists in conclusions are clearly stated	1,2,3
5	Potential options and solutions are identified and evaluated for their contribution to improving cost ratios and revenue generation	2,3,4
6	Recommendations to inform decisions are based on clearly stated conclusions drawn from an accurate analysis of all relevant information	2,3,4
7	Recommendations are presented to the appropriate people in a clear and concise way and are supported with a clear rationale	1,2,3,4

THE SITUATION

Your name is Nathan King and you are employed by the Engineering Research Council (ERC) as a project analyst to work on their Waste Reduction Programme. The purpose of this programme is to fund projects that are proposed jointly by academic and commercial partners to develop and exploit technology that will reduce the amount of industrial waste going to landfill. Ideally, projects should be capable of commercialisation on a scale beyond that of solving the problems of the commercial partner. The commercial partner must also provide a part of the funding. Your role is to undertake an initial screening of the outline proposals, and to assist the partners in the preparation of more detailed plans for evaluation by the Project Management Committee who will make the funding decisions.

You are currently working on a proposal that has been put forward by Derwent University and Allbright Metals plc.

Organisations involved in the simulation

Engineering Research Council
Derwent University
Allbright Metals plc

Personnel involved in the simulation

Nathan King	Project Analyst, ERC
Professor Z Goran	Professor of Engineering, Derwent University
Ian Stewart	Managing Director, Allbright Metals Ltd
Katy Williams	Secretary to Ian Stewart, Allbright Metals Ltd
Angela Ellis	Production Director, Allbright Metals Ltd

THE TASKS TO BE COMPLETED

1 Refer to the ERC guidelines on allowable expenditure and Section 2 of the outline proposal that deals with the Derwent University research costings.

    (a) Identify which of the costs included by Derwent University should be disallowed.

    (b) Redraft the cost statement to meet ERC guidelines.

    (c) Write a memo to Professor Goran at Derwent University explaining what you have done and the accounting principles involved. You should also highlight how much the likely research element of any grant awarded for the project would be and summarise the changes that have been made to the budget.

2 Professor Goran and Katy Williams have worked together to produce some estimates of the cost of building and operating the pilot plant. These are included in Section 3 of the outline proposal. You are required to:

    (a) Estimate the cost of the pilot plant according to ERC guidelines. The effective rate of corporation tax paid by Allbright Metals is 30%, and it can be assumed that corporation tax is paid one year in arrears.

    (b) Calculate by how much the annual savings in waste disposal costs would need to increase for the pilot plant to breakeven at the end of four years in operational terms, excluding capital costs, tax and NPV effects.

3 The Project Management Committee have asked you to make an assessment of the commercial viability of the process on a larger scale. The Production Director at Allbright Metals has provided you with some figures on the varying costs of the different types of

waste disposal that are involved in the existing and new processes. These are contained in the fax, shown later in the Assessment. Section 4 of the outline proposal sets out the effect of the new process on the tonnages of the different types of waste going to landfill, and Section 5 provides estimates of the costs of operating the new plant on a commercial scale. Appendix 1 provides an extract from the relevant part of the overhead cost budget for Allbright Metals should the full-scale plant be built.

You are required to:

(a) Calculate the saving in waste disposal costs per tonne of material going into the new process

(b) Calculate the income per tonne of material going into the new process, arising from the sale of recovered metals

(c) Prepare a budgeted annual cost statement for the process on a total cost basis and on a cost per tonne of inputs basis, using the most likely landfill tax rate and lead price. Use this to assess the likely profitability of the process

(d) Find the effect on the budgeted profit of the possible alternative landfill tax rate and lead price, and calculate the probable outcome

(e) Draft a brief note for the Project Management Committee giving your views on the commercial viability of the process

4   Ian Stewart is considering the possibility of processing sludge produced by other metallurgical companies in the region on a commercial basis, but is unsure as to the basis on which such a service should be priced. He has asked you for your views on the implications of such a development. Draft a fax to Ian Stewart outlining both the commercial and non-commercial factors that might influence this decision.

DERWENT UNIVERSITY – ALLBRIGHT METALS LTD
IRON AND LEAD EXTRACTION PROJECT

Section 1: Project summary

Allbright Metals Ltd is a small family-owned manufacturing business. It uses a metal cutting process that produces a wet sludge, which is currently classified as a 'special waste'. Special wastes are subject to strict control by the Environment Agency and this particular sludge is difficult and expensive to dispose of. The Engineering Department at Derwent University has been working on the recovery of metals from liquids and sludges, and preliminary trials suggest that two of their technologies could be appropriate to the Allbright Metals situation.

The technologies to be developed involve the following three processes.

1   Magnetic separation to remove the iron from the sludge.

2   Filtration using a membrane to remove the lead from the sludge.

3   Further filtration and compaction to produce an inert semi-solid material that would be appropriate for landfill.

The project would be funded jointly by the ERC and Allbright Metals. It is proposed that the ERC should pay the research costs, plus 20% of the cost of building the pilot plant. If the project is successful, Allbright Metals will seek to offer the treatment on a commercial basis to other metallurgical companies.

Section 2: Research budget

	£	Note
Research staff costs:		1
Project Director	30,000	2
Researcher 1	16,000	
Researcher 2	14,000	
Sub-total	60,000	
Expenses:		
Lab technician's salary	11,000	3
Laboratory consumables	5,000	
IT department overhead apportionment	1,200	
Library apportionment	800	
Departmental overhead	2,300	
Travel	800	
Conferences	2,300	
Training	1,800	4
Secretary's salary	10,000	
Administrator's salary	10,000	
Laboratory refurbishment	6,000	5
Purchase of filtration equipment	3,500	
Adaptation of compactor	2,200	6
Purchase of magnetic separator	15,000	
Sub-total	71,900	
Total	131,900	

Notes

1   All salaries shown are the annual gross pay of the individual concerned. National Insurance has been excluded, but this is estimated as 10% of the annual salary.

2   It is estimated that the Project Director will spend 25% of his time on the project.

3   The Lab Technician will be recruited for the project, but will spend 50% of his time on other duties.

4   The training cost include an item of £750, which is the cost of supervising the second researcher for his masters' degree.

5   A laboratory that is currently used for teaching purposes will need to be refurbished prior to its allocation to the project.

6   An existing compactor will be modified to make it appropriate for use on this project.

Section 3: Pilot plant proposals

A pilot plant will be built at Allbright Metals by engineering staff employed by the company. The labour cost involved will be paid by Allbright Metals as part of their contribution to the funding, and these costs will therefore be recorded separately. The costs for which ERC funding is sought are as follows.

1   The cost of the capital equipment (all to be purchased at the start of the project). This amounts to £30,000, and capital allowances will be available at the rate of 25% on a reducing balance basis. It is expected that the pilot plant will have a life of four years, at the end of which time it will be scrapped.

2   A feasibility study was carried out by an independent consultant for the price of £5,000.

3   The cost of operating the plant:

(a)   Labour – the cost of one skilled production operative at £10,000 per year. There is a collective pay agreement in force at the plant that links pay rises to the regional metallurgical workers pay index, which for the last year stood at 135. The index is expected to move as follows over the next four years:

Year 1	139
Year 2	144
Year 3	149
Year 4	155

(b)   The cost of power is expected to be £1,200 in year 1 and £1,500 per year thereafter.

(c)   Replacement membranes will be required monthly (12 per year) in the first year, and at twice this rate thereafter. This is in excess of the expected eventual usage to allow regular sampling and analysis. A four-year contract for the supply of the membranes has been negotiated at the fixed price of £250 per membrane.

4   The pilot plant is expected to reduce waste disposal costs by £11,000 per year.

5   The pilot plant will occupy 1,000 square feet in a currently unoccupied part of the factory. Rent and rates amount to £5.50 per square foot.

Section 4: Effects on disposal tonnages

The amount of wet sludge currently produced per year by Allbright Metals is approximately 2,000 tonnes. This is currently all disposed of to a waste disposal contractor. Outputs from the new process will be:

•   200 tonnes of an iron rich compound that will be sold to a metal reprocessing company

•   400 tonnes of a lead-containing compound that will be sold to a metal reprocessing company

•   1,000 tonnes of inert compacted material that can be disposed of to landfill

•   A large volume of effluent. The composition of the effluent would allow it to be disposed of to sewer within the terms of the current discharge consent, and this would therefore not incur any additional costs

Section 5: Cost of commercial scale operation

To operate the plant on a commercial basis will incur the following costs.

1   A supervisor who currently works on the main production unit would be transferred to the new process. He earns £14,000 per year, and would be replaced in the main production unit by a new employee on a similar wage level.

2   Three semi-skilled operatives would be recruited on a wage level of £9,500 per year.

3   The magnetic separator involves significant inputs of electricity, and a new supply would be provided for the plant, which would be separately metered. The contract with Northshire Electricity plc relates the price per unit to the total units supplied according to the graph below.

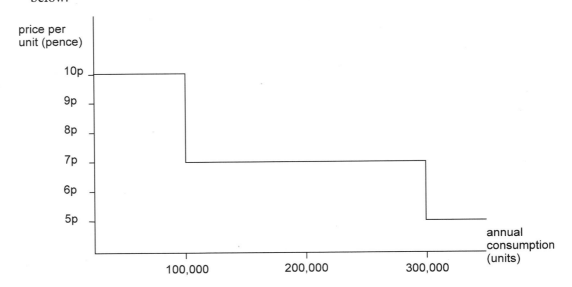

4   The electricity requirement is 100 units per tonne of inputs.

5   The contract for membranes negotiated for the pilot plant will be continued. It is estimated that each membrane will have a life of 100 tonnes of inputs.

6   Depreciation is estimated at £4,000 per year.

7   The plant will occupy 2,000 square feet of space.

8   Direct labour hours are expected to be 7,000 per year, and machine hours are expected to be 1,800 per year.

Appendix 1: Extract from production overhead budget

Indirect labour	£35,000
Maintenance labour	£54,000
Maintenance materials	£90,000
Other production overhead	£74,000

Indirect labour costs are allocated to the production departments on the basis of direct labour hours. Total budgeted direct labour hours including the new process are 70,000.

Total machine hours are budgeted to be 72,000, including the new process.

Other production overhead is allocated on the basis of floor space occupied. Total factory floor space is 20,000 square feet.

ALLBRIGHT METALS LTD
FAX TRANSMISSION

To: Nathan King, Environmental Research Council
From: Angela Ellis, Production Director
Date: dd.mm.yy
Subject: Waste disposal prices

Further to our telephone conversation, I can confirm that the current price paid for the disposal of metal-containing sludge is £50 per tonne. There is a contract in place with Cleanup plc, a waste disposal contractor, to collect the sludge from the plant on a daily basis. Cleanup take the sludge to their liquid waste treatment facility where it is processed prior to disposal, subject to controls enforced by the Environment Agency. The contract requires a three-month notice period to be given prior to termination, but obviously we would be able to give ample notice if we did decide to go ahead and build a full-scale facility.

The inert compacted material that would be produced by the new process would not be subject to the special waste regulations and would not require further treatment prior to landfill. Cleanup has quoted a price of £12 per tonne, including landfill tax of £2 per tonne, for the collection and disposal of this waste. I have discussed the landfill tax implications with the Commercial Director of Cleanup, who believes that the government are likely to raise the level of tax on inert waste to a level comparable with that on other waste. He is also of the opinion that the level of landfill tax is likely to increase significantly over the next few years, believing that there is a 40% chance that all forms of waste going to landfill could be taxed at the rate of £15 per tonne within a couple of years. Surprisingly, no such tax is paid on our existing liquid waste because this is discharged to sewer after treatment at Cleanup's facility.

I have also been in contact with some metal reprocessing companies to establish a rough level of income that we might expect to receive for the sale of the recovered metals. They estimate that the iron-containing material might attract a price of £5 per tonne, depending on the quality of the material, and the lead-containing compound would realise perhaps £6 per tonne. However, until they receive samples of the lead-containing compound they cannot quote a firm price, and the £6 price is at the conservative end of the scale. It is possible that if the lead is easily recoverable the price could be as high as £20 per tonne. I estimate that there is a 25% chance that we could realise this price in practice.

I can confirm that the terms of our discharge consent would permit the effluent produced by the process to be disposed of to sewer without additional cost.

Please do not hesitate to contact me if you would like any further information.

ENGINEERING RESEARCH COUNCIL – WASTE REDUCTION PROGRAMME GUIDELINES FOR ALLOWABLE EXPENDITURE

1   **Research expenditure**

Only expenditure that is incurred directly as a result of undertaking the project will be allowed. Costs should be grouped into the following categories:

- Salary costs
- Expenses
- Capital costs

Costs that may be charged to the project include:

- The costs of the research staff involved in the project, in proportion to the time spent. These costs include their salary payments, National Insurance, and any pension contributions paid by the employer

- The costs of the Project Director, apportioned on a time basis as for the research staff

- The costs of technicians, apportioned on a time basis as for the research staff

- Travel expenses of the staff involved

- Training and conference costs for research staff where courses or conferences are directly relevant to the project

- Laboratory consumables purchased for the project

- The cost of any capital equipment purchased for the project, or the cost of refurbishment or alterations to existing capital equipment for the purpose of the project

- Overheads will be allowed at a rate of 40% of the total research staff budget (excluding technicians, but including the Project Director)

Costs that may not be charged to the project include:

- Apportionment of administrative staff costs
- Laboratory power, light and heat
- General property improvements
- Apportionment of other service department costs and overheads

2   **Pilot plant expenditure**

- Only the costs directly incurred in the building and operation of pilot plant will be allowed.

- Cost savings that result from pilot plant operation must be credited to the project.

- Capital allowances and corporation tax effects must be taken into account in calculating costs. It should be assumed that all tax losses will be realisable.

- Projects should be evaluated using net present value techniques, with a discount rate of 20%.

- Three-digit discount tables, reproduced below, should be used in determining net present values.

- Any initial capital outlay should be shown as taking place in year 0.

- Operating cashflows should be treated as occurring at the year-end.

Discount rate at end of year	*10%*	*15%*	*20%*	*25%*
1	0.909	0.870	0.833	0.800
2	0.826	0.756	0.694	0.640
3	0.751	0.658	0.579	0.512
4	0.683	0.572	0.482	0.410
5	0.621	0.497	0.402	0.328
6	0.564	0.432	0.335	0.262
7	0.513	0.376	0.279	0.210
8	0.467	0.327	0.233	0.168
9	0.424	0.284	0.194	0.134
10	0.386	0.247	0.162	0.107

TRIAL RUN DEVOLVED ASSESSMENT 2

NORTHOVER SCHOOL

Coverage of performance criteria

Element 16.1: Prepare cost estimates	Tasks
1 The extent of the information to be contained within estimates is agreed with those who commission them	2, 3
2 Appropriate staff are consulted about technical aspects and any special features of work activity and projects which impact upon costs	2, 3
3 Current material, labour and other variable costs are identified and future trends assessed	1, 2, 3, 4
4 Estimates account for the effect of possible variations in capacity on fixed overhead rates	3
5 Estimates are prepared in an approved form and presented to the appropriate people within an agreed timescale	1, 2, 3

Element 16.2: Recommend ways to improve cost ratios and revenue generation	
1 Information relevant to estimating current and future costs and revenue is identified and used as the basis of analysis	1, 2, 3, 4
2 Critical factors which may affect costs and revenue are analysed using appropriate accounting techniques and clear conclusions are drawn from the analysis	2, 3, 4
3 The views of appropriate specialists are gathered and used to inform analysis and any conclusions drawn	1, 2, 3
4 The assumptions made and the degree of accuracy which exists in conclusions are clearly stated	3
5 Potential options and solutions are identified and evaluated for their contribution to improving cost ratios and revenue generation	2, 3
6 Recommendations to inform decisions are based on clearly stated conclusions drawn from an accurate analysis of all relevant information	1, 2, 3
7 Recommendations are presented to the appropriate people in a clear and concise way and are supported with a clear rationale	2, 3, 4

THE SITUATION

Your name is Chetna Paul and you work for the Solent Local Education Authority (LEA) as a school budget co-ordinator. Although budget responsibility is now devolved to school governors, your role is to work with head-teachers on the detailed planning of school finances.

Solent LEA is in the process of changing the age at which pupils transfer from one school to another in order to bring it into line with the majority of LEAs in England and Wales. At present, Solent pupils enter a first school at the age of five, transfer to middle school at the age of eight (end of Year 3), and move on to secondary school at the age of twelve (end of Year 7). In future, although the age of first school entry will be unchanged, pupils will transfer to middle school when they are seven (end of Year 2), and to secondary school at the age of eleven (end of Year 6). This change in policy has severe repercussions on the budgets of the first and middle schools, which governors are attempting to resolve in a variety of ways. You are currently working with Northover First School as it seeks to address these issues. Under the existing arrangements, Northover First School has children in four different year groups – Reception, Year 1, Year 2 and Year 3 – with two classes per year group.

Organisations involved in the simulation:

Solent Local Education Authority
Solent County Council
Northover First School

Personnel involved in the simulation:

Chetna Paul	School Budget Co-ordinator, Solent LEA
Mrs Susan Parker	Headteacher, Northover First School
Sharon Coates	School Secretary, Northover First School
Alan Peskett	Head of Pre-school Education, Solent LEA
Joan Fairfax	County Architect, Solent County Council
Roger Austin	Director of Education, Solent LEA

THE TASKS TO BE COMPLETED

1 The current year budget for Northover First School can be found below. Assuming that no changes are made to the budgeted costs and revenues other than those indicated in the extract from the Budget Guidelines, make a first draft of the next year's budget and calculate whether the school will be financially viable for the coming educational year. It can be assumed that the redundancy costs will be taken in the current year.

2 Study the information contained in the memos from Mrs Parker and from Sharon Coates.

    (a) Redraft the figures submitted by Sharon Coates to show the real effect on the school budget of operating a nursery class. Current year figures can be used for this purpose.

    (b) Write a memo to Mrs Parker giving your views on the financial viability of the proposals and their impact on the financial position of the school.

3 Undertake the calculations requested in the memo from Roger Austin to you. Draft a reply which answers his queries on the pricing issue.

4 You receive a telephone call from Sharon Coates to let you know that the local toddler group has approached Mrs Parker with a request to use both the spare classrooms on a

Tuesday morning at a cost of £20 per week. If they cannot use both rooms then they will have to look for alternative premises. She wishes to know whether this will make a difference to the financial evaluation of the pre-school class proposals. Write a memo in reply that explains the accounting implications of such an offer.

NORTHOVER FIRST SCHOOL - CURRENT YEAR BUDGET

Number of children per year		75
Number of children on roll		300
LEA funding per child (capitation)		£900
Special needs budget		£16,000
Number of classes		8

	Notes	£	
LEA funding:			
Capitation			270,000
Special needs			16,000
Sub-total			286,000
Teaching staff:			
Headteacher		29,000	
Deputy headteacher		25,000	
Grade 7 teachers (£20,000 per year) × 2	1	40,000	
Grade 5 teachers (£18,000 per year) × 2		36,000	
Grade 3 teachers (£15,000 per year) × 3	1	45,000	
Sub-total			175,000
Ancillary staff:			
Classroom assistants (£10,000 per year) × 4	1	40,000	
Secretary		11,000	
Caretaker		10,000	
Sub-total			61,000
Other costs:			
Stationery	2	15,000	
Books & other resources	3	9,000	
IT support	4	4,000	
Heating	4	5,000	
Cleaning	4	6,000	
Maintenance	4	4,000	
Sundry	4	5,000	
Sub-total			48,000
Total costs			284,000
Budget surplus			2,000

Notes

1   One Grade 5 teacher, one Grade 3 teacher and one classroom assistant will be made redundant when the Year 3 pupils are lost to the middle school.

2   Stationery costs are semi-variable, with a fixed element of £3,000 per annum.

3   The cost of books and other resources is fully variable.

4   All remaining costs are fixed.

MEMO

Date: dd.mm.yy

To: Chetna Paul
               Solent Local Education Authority

From: Mrs S Parker
               Northover First School

Subject: Pre-school Class proposals

As you will be aware, it seems unlikely that my school will continue to be able to operate without significant changes once the Year 3 pupils have been transferred to the middle school. The Policy Adviser at the LEA has suggested that we could consider opening a pre-school class for four year olds, which would form part of the LEA strategy for extending the availability of pre-school education in line with government policy.

Although the costs of building modifications and new equipment would be met from LEA funds, I still think it is unlikely that such a course of action would solve our financial problems. This is primarily because we would be required to maintain a staff:pupil ratio of 1:12. In addition, a local survey of parents suggests that although in theory we could offer 48 places by using the two Year 3 classrooms that will be empty, in practice we could not fill more than 30 places due to competition with other pre-school providers. As a result, I believe that if we do go down this route, we should operate a single class of 24 children that would be run by an NNEB qualified playleader. She would be assisted by students on secondment from the local College of Further Education who require pre-school placements as a part of their Diploma in Childcare course. These assistants would not therefore be salaried.

My secretary, Sharon Coates, will be providing you with some figures, and I would appreciate your views once you have had an opportunity to study them. I have asked her to assume a capitation of £1,000 per child at the suggestion of the Policy Adviser.

MEMO

Date: dd.mm.yy

To: Chetna Paul
               Solent Local Education Authority

From: Sharon Coates
               Northover First School

Subject: Pre-school Class proposals

I have calculated the effect on the budget of operating a pre-school class, and the figures are attached. I have not had much experience of this type of work before and so I will explain how I have arrived at some of the figures.

1   When the pre-school class is in place and the Year 3 pupils have left we will have a total of seven classes in the school. I have therefore apportioned the following costs on this basis:

- Headteacher's salary
- Secretary's salary
- Caretaker's salary
- Heating

- Cleaning
- Maintenance
- Sundry

2   I have not apportioned the cost of the Deputy Head because she also acts as a full time class teacher.

3   In the main budget, stationery costs are semi-variable and so I have included the £3,000 fixed element plus the variable element based on the number of pupils as in the main budget.

4   I have included the cost of books at the same rate as in the main budget.

5   Mrs Parker tells me that we should expect to recruit an experienced playleader on a salary of £15,000 per year.

I hope this is correct. Please let me know if you would like me to make any revisions to the calculations.

NORTHOVER FIRST SCHOOL - PRE-SCHOOL CLASS BUDGET

Number of children per year		24
LEA funding per child (capitation)		£1,000
Special needs budget		£0
Number of classes		1
		£
LEA funding:		
Capitation		24,000
Special needs		0
Sub-total		24,000
Teaching staff:		
Headteacher	4,143	
Playleader	15,000	
Sub-total		19,143
Ancillary staff:		
Secretary	1,571	
Caretaker	1,429	
Sub-total		3,000
Other costs:		
Stationery	3,960	
Books & other resources	720	
Heating	714	
Cleaning	857	
Maintenance	571	
Sundry	714	
Sub-total		7,536
Total costs		29,679
Budget deficit		-5,679

SOLENT LOCAL EDUCATION AUTHORITY

MEMO

Date: dd.mm.yy
To: Chetna Paul, School Budget Co-ordinator
From: Roger Austin, Director of Education
Subject: Extension of nursery provision

As you will know, all the Local Education Authorities are currently looking at ways in which they might extend the provision of nursery places to three year olds. I have been in discussions about this with Alan Peskett and he has produced some proposals for a pilot scheme in one of the schools that you deal with, Northover First School. I would be grateful if you would take some time to study the attached briefing paper and memo from the County Architect and provide me with a financial evaluation of their proposals in accordance with budget guidelines. I would particularly like you to address the following issues:

1   What the annual revenue budget for the project would look like.

2   What price we would have to charge parents per session for the class to breakeven.

3   The payback period for the project.

4   The NPV cost or benefit of the proposals over five years. You can exclude inflation in your preliminary calculations.

5   One of the elected members of the County Council has also discussed these proposals with me, and her view is that once Solent starts to offer nursery and pre-school places in primary schools, demand will increase massively as parents realise the additional benefits that school can offer. Given that in a purpose built unit we can accommodate 20 three year olds in a classroom or 24 four year olds, and assuming that session prices and LEA funding rates for four year olds remain the same, which age group should we concentrate on to achieve the best financial results?

6   What do you think are the main sensitivities in the proposal?

I would also be interested to have your views on the approaches that we could take in deciding how much to charge parents per session.

SOLENT LOCAL EDUCATION AUTHORITY

BRIEFING PAPER

Date: dd.mm.yy
To: Director of Education
From: Head of Pre-school Education
Subject: Extension of nursery provision

As you know, the DfEE have asked us to draft proposals for extending the provision of LEA run nursery places to three-year-olds. I believe that in the Solent LEA an opportunity currently exists to increase the number of places available without incurring large capital costs. This is possible because the change in the age of transfer of children from first to middle school means that the first schools will have spare classrooms available once they have lost their Year 3 pupils. This will not be feasible in all cases due to the different building requirements and health and safety regulations that apply to nurseries for younger children, and also because some of the first schools have come up with alternative plans for their spare capacity. However, I do think that we should pursue this possibility further and I have made a detailed study of the situation in one school, Northover First School, which I believe could be used to develop a model for the extension of nursery places in the Solent area.

Northover is currently considering offering places to four-year-olds, but their plans would still leave one classroom unused. Due to the more stringent building regulations and health and safety rules that apply to premises used as nurseries for three year olds, some building modifications would be required, and I have asked the County Architect to draw up some preliminary plans and costings for these.

I have put together some figures that might form the basis of a revenue budget for the project, which are detailed below. The nursery would offer two three hour sessions per day, and the cost to parents per session should probably be around £4.50. The nursery would follow the current school year of 39 weeks. My researches suggest that prices in the area range from £2.50 to £6.25 per session, depending on the type of services offered by the nursery.

If we operate on a staff:pupil ratio of 1:6 we could offer eighteen places in the space available. Staffing at each session would be a playleader who would be responsible for all aspects of running the class, and who would report to the playleader in the class for four-year-olds, an assistant and a student on placement from the College of Further Education.

Running costs:

Playleader	£14,000 per year
Assistant	£4.50 per hour
Student	No cost
Stationery	50p per child per session
Other resources	25p per child per session
Additional heating and cleaning	£7.00 per day

In addition we would have to invest in new play equipment, which would cost in the region of £3,000, and furniture at a cost of £2,500.

I look forward to receiving your comments on my proposals.

SOLENT COUNTY COUNCIL

MEMO

Date:	dd.mm.yy
To:	Alan Peskett, Head of Pre-school Education Solent Local Education Authority
From:	Joan Fairfax, County Architect
Subject:	Proposed building modifications to Northover First School

Further to our telephone conversation, I have consulted the regulations and visited the school in question. I have drawn up some preliminary plans for the work that would be required which we can discuss at the liaison meeting on Thursday. I have also consulted with the Surveyors Department to give you some idea of the costs involved, which are as follows:

1	Modifications to cloakroom area	£1,000
2	Installation of additional toilets	£1,500
3	Redesign of entrances and exits	£1,500
4	Additional fencing and security	£3,000
5	Redecoration	£1,000

The redecoration costs are known since this forms part of the routine maintenance programme and is scheduled to be carried out in any event next term.

SOLENT LOCAL EDUCATION AUTHORITY

BUDGET GUIDELINES (EXTRACTS)

Section 3: Salary rises

1 Teaching staff salaries are subject to a national agreement on teachers' pay. For budget purposes, it should be assumed that salaries will rise by 3% next year.

2 Ancillary staff pay is governed by an agreement that links salaries to the regional service sector pay index. The index currently stands at 160, and it is expected to be 165 next year.

Section 5: Capitation

1 The capitation has been set at £920 per primary school pupil up to and including year 6, and at £1,550 per secondary school pupil from year 7 upwards.

Section 8: Pre-school Classes

The cost of resources for pre-school classes will be different from those in the rest of the primary sector:

1 Stationery costs will be £30 per head.
2 Books and other resources will be budgeted at £15 per head.
3 IT support should be budgeted at the rate of £1,000 per class.

Section 10: Evaluation of capital expenditure

1 Projects should be evaluated using net present value techniques, with a discount rate of 15%.

2 Three-digit discount tables, reproduced below, should be used in determining net present values.

3 Any initial capital outlay should be shown as taking place in year 0.

4 Revenue cash flows should be treated as occurring at the year-end.

5 Any income that is received as a direct result of undertaking the project should be credited to the project.

Discount rate at end of year	10%	15%	20%	25%
1	0.909	0.870	0.833	0.800
2	0.826	0.756	0.694	0.640
3	0.751	0.658	0.579	0.512
4	0.683	0.572	0.482	0.410
5	0.621	0.497	0.402	0.328
6	0.564	0.432	0.335	0.262
7	0.513	0.376	0.279	0.210
8	0.467	0.327	0.233	0.168
9	0.424	0.284	0.194	0.134
10	0.386	0.247	0.162	0.107

BPP PUBLISHING

AAT Sample
Simulation

AAT SAMPLE SIMULATION

Coverage of performance criteria

Element 16.1: Prepare cost estimates	Tasks
1 The extent of the information to be contained within estimates is agreed with those who commission them	1, 2, 3, 4, 5
2 Appropriate staff are consulted about technical aspects and any special features of work activity and projects which impact upon costs	1, 2, 3, 4, 5
3 Current material, labour and other variable costs are identified and future trends assessed	1, 2, 3, 4, 5
4 Estimates account for the effect of possible variations in capacity on fixed overhead rates	3
5 Estimates are prepared in an approved form and presented to the appropriate people within an agreed timescale	1, 2, 3, 4, 5
Element 16.2: Recommend ways to improve cost ratios and revenue generation	
1 Information relevant to estimating current and future costs and revenue is identified and used as the basis of analysis	1, 2, 3, 4, 5
2 Critical factors which may affect costs and revenue are analysed using appropriate accounting techniques and clear conclusions are drawn from the analysis	1, 2, 3, 4, 5
3 The views of appropriate specialists are gathered and used to inform analysis and any conclusions drawn	1, 2, 3, 4, 5
4 The assumptions made and the degree of accuracy which exists in conclusions are clearly stated	1, 2, 3, 4, 5
5 Potential options and solutions are identified and evaluated for their contribution to improving cost ratios and revenue generation	2, 3, 4, 5
6 Recommendations to inform decisions are based on clearly stated conclusions drawn from an accurate analysis of all relevant information	1, 2, 3, 4, 5
7 Recommendations are presented to the appropriate people in a clear and concise way and are supported with a clear rationale	1, 2, 3, 4, 5

INSTRUCTIONS

This simulation is designed to test your ability to evaluate current and proposed activities.

*You are allowed **four hours** to complete your work.*

A high level of accuracy is required. Check your work carefully.

Correcting fluid may be used but it should be used in moderation. Any errors should be crossed out neatly and clearly. The use of pencils for your written answers is not acceptable.

You should read the whole simulation before commencing work so as to gain an overall picture of what is required.

THE SITUATION

Your name is Sally Parkin and you are employed as a financial analyst with the Midtown Enterprise Agency. The agency provides technical, marketing and financial assistance to small- and medium-sized businesses in Midtown and surrounding areas. Each company which registers with the agency is assigned a counsellor who attends board meetings and offers advice and guidance. Companies registered with the agency can also call on its services at any time.

One company regularly calling on the services of the agency is Questking Ltd. Neil Henderson, a counsellor employed by the Midtown Enterprise Agency, was allocated Questking Ltd as a client some 12 months ago. Since becoming involved with Questking, you have made several visits to the company and have access to the company's accounting procedures manual.

Organisations involved in the simulation

Midtown Enterprise Agency
Questking Ltd

Personnel involved in the simulation

Financial analyst to the agency	Yourself, Sally Parkin
Counsellor responsible for Questking Ltd	Neil Henderson
Managing Director of Questking Ltd	Helen Johnson
Production Director of Questking Ltd	Tony Anderson
Marketing Director of Questking Ltd	Ann Fowler
Company Secretary of Questking Ltd	John Peters

The company's products and organisation

Questking Ltd has four divisions. Division A is located on a separate site and produces and sells a modem used in computers. This is its only product. Divisions B, C and D share the same site. This site comprises a single factory where divisions B, C and D are located plus a central office block containing the personnel, finance and administration functions. Division B makes four products, P1, P2, P3 and P4. Divisions C and D each make a single product.

THE TASKS TO BE COMPLETED

Before commencing the tasks, read the extract from the accounting procedures manual of Questking Ltd later in the simulation, the memo from your colleague, Neil Henderson and the agenda for the board meeting.

Some suggested answer formats are provided but you may prefer to use another format with which you are familiar.

Task 1

Refer to the memo from Ann Fowler, the marketing director, Annex 2, and to Annex 1.1.

- Identify those costs which would be saved and those costs which would still be incurred if Division C were to be closed.

- Use your findings to identify the change in Questking Ltd's profit if Division C is closed.

- Prepare brief notes for Neil Henderson stating and justifying your recommendation for the future of Division C.

- Using the data in Annex 1.1, identify one limitation to your recommendation.

The budget for Division C has been reproduced and a possible answer format provided later in the simulation.

Task 2

Refer to the memo from Tony Anderson, the production director, and the budget for Division B (shown as Annex 1.3).

- Calculate a revised production schedule which will maximise the profits of Division B for the forthcoming year.

- Identify the total contribution made by your proposal.

- Show the change in profit compared with the proposal by Tony Anderson.

- Suggest one commercial reason why your proposal might not be accepted.

A possible format is provided later in the simulation.

Task 3

Refer to the letter from Neil Henderson to Helen Johnson, the managing director of Questking Ltd, and the budget for Division A (shown as Annex 1.2).

- Calculate the existing quarterly fixed and unit variable costs included in the cost of labour.

- Identify the existing total cost of fixed production overheads per quarter.

- Calculate the existing quarterly break-even point using the fixed costs directly attributable to Division A.

- Use your answer to identify the quarter in which Division A would begin to adversely affect Questking's overall profit, assuming current trends continue.

- Recalculate the quarterly break-even point using the revised costing proposed by Neil Henderson.

- Show the change in profit for the year if Neil Henderson's proposals are accepted and recommend whether or not his proposal should be accepted.

Your answer should be prepared in the format shown later in the simulation.

Task 4

Refer to that part of Neil Henderson's memo relating to the order from Past Computers Ltd and the memo from Ann Fowler, the marketing director.

- Use the data given in Annex 1.2 concerning fixed production overhead absorbed and unabsorbed and the explanation of accounting policies given to calculate the maximum capacity of Division A and any surplus capacity.

- Use your findings to evaluate the special order from Past Computers detailed in the memo from Ann Fowler, the marketing director. You should also refer to the memo from Neil Henderson to evaluate the three options identified and make a recommendation whether or not to accept the special order.

- Write a memo to Neil Henderson. Your memo should summarise the profitability of the three options, suggest which option to take and identify *one* non-financial, commercial factor which should also be considered.

Task 5

Refer to the memo from John Peters, the company secretary, the contract document ('Invitation to tender') and the extract from the accounting procedures manual.

- Evaluate the proposal using the net present value technique.

- Justify your treatment of the £80,000 sales proceeds of the existing machine.

For your evaluation you may wish to use the form used by the Midtown Enterprise Agency for evaluating clients' investment proposals, a copy of which appears in the 'suggested formats for answers' later in the simulation.

MIDTOWN ENTERPRISE AGENCY

INTERNAL MEMO

Date: 1 December

To: Sally Parkin

From: Neil Henderson

Subject: Board meeting at Questking Ltd

I have just received the agenda and other papers for the board meeting at Questking Ltd to be held on 12 December. Unfortunately, I will be away from the office working with another client for the next 8 days. As you have helped Questking in the past, would you be good enough to read through the documents and prepare notes for me to use at the board meeting?

The possibility of a contract with Past Computers really cannot wait until the board meeting. If we are going to accept the contract we ought not to delay it as the company would be a prestigious customer.

Because of this, I guess that Questking will want to accept the contract even if it does make a loss.

There appear to be three options:

• source the full contract from internal production
• subcontract the whole order to Bright Processors Ltd
• a mixture of in-house production and subcontracting

Can you therefore write me a memo evaluating these three options for me to read when I return to the office. As I need this information before the board meeting, you should use the existing cost data for Division A and *not* my proposed changes.

Many thanks.

QUESTKING LTD

Mill Road, Midtown MX14 8XY

29 November

To members of the board of directors

Board meeting

The next board meeting will take place in the board room at Mill Road on 12 December at 10.00 am. A buffet lunch will be served at 12.30 pm.

Chair: Helen Johnson, Managing Director

Board members: Tony Anderson - Production Director
                           Ann Fowler - Marketing Director
                           John Peters - Company Secretary

In attendance: Neil Henderson - Midtown Enterprise Agency

Agenda

1	Apologies for absence	
2	Minutes of the previous meeting	to be tabled
3	Matters arising from the minutes	
4	Consideration of the budget for the next financial year	Annex 1.1 - 1.3
5	The future of Division C	Annex 2
6	Fire at Modern Suppliers Ltd - implications for Questking Ltd	Annex 3
7	The strategic development of Division A	Annex 4
8	Special order from Past Computers Ltd	Annex 5
9	Possible contract with Meldreth plc	Annex 6 - 7
10	Any other business	

John Peters

Company Secretary

Annex 1.1

QUESTKING LTD
COMPANY BUDGETED PROFIT STATEMENT FOR NEXT YEAR

Division	A	B	C	D	Total
	£	£	£	£	£
Turnover	1,500,000	2,170,000	2,240,000	1,950,500	7,860,500
Material	660,000	609,000	789,000	690,400	2,748,400
Labour	357,000	310,200	524,100	387,100	1,578,400
Light, heat and power	80,000	120,000	150,000	90,000	440,000
Rent	50,000	160,000	200,000	120,000	530,000
Rates	30,000	240,000	300,000	180,000	750,000
Sales commission	75,000	108,500	112,000	97,525	393,025
Selling expenses	60,000	88,000	140,800	83,400	372,200
Central overheads					
Personnel	34,000	64,000	102,400	62,100	262,500
Finance	18,000	48,000	76,800	46,575	189,375
Administration	22,000	96,000	42,500	21,400	181,900
Profit/(loss)	114,000	326,300	(197,600)	172,000	414,700

Annex 1.2

DIVISION A
DIVISIONAL BUDGETED PROFIT FOR NEXT YEAR BY QUARTER

	Quarter 1	Quarter 2	Quarter 3	Quarter 4	Total
Units produced and sold	9,000	8,000	7,000	6,000	30,000
	£	£	£	£	£
Turnover	450,000	400,000	350,000	300,000	1,500,000
Material	198,000	176,000	154,000	132,000	660,000
Labour	97,500	92,000	86,500	81,000	357,000
Fixed production overhead absorbed	36,000	32,000	28,000	24,000	120,000
Gross profit	118,500	100,000	81,500	63,000	363,000
Sales commission	22,500	20,000	17,500	15,000	75,000
Fixed production overhead unabsorbed	4,000	8,000	12,000	16,000	40,000
Selling expenses	15,000	15,000	15,000	15,000	60,000
Central overheads					
Personnel	8,500	8,500	8,500	8,500	34,000
Finance	4,500	4,500	4,500	4,500	18,000
Administration	5,500	5,500	5,500	5,500	22,000
Net profit/(loss)	58,500	38,500	18,500	(1,500)	114,000

Annex 1.3

DIVISION B
BUDGETED PROFIT STATEMENT FOR NEXT YEAR BY PRODUCT

Product	P1	P2	P3	P4	Total
Units	1,900	2,600	2,000	1,500	8,000
	£	£	£	£	£
Turnover	380,000	650,000	600,000	540,000	2,170,000
Material	114,000	195,000	120,000	180,000	609,000
Labour	45,600	93,600	144,000	27,000	310,200
Light, heat and power	28,500	39,000	30,000	22,500	120,000
Rent	20,000	10,000	100,000	30,000	160,000
Rates	30,000	15,000	150,000	45,000	240,000
Sales commission	19,000	32,500	30,000	27,000	108,500
Selling expenses	20,900	28,600	22,000	16,500	88,000
Central overheads					
Personnel	15,200	20,800	16,000	12,000	64,000
Finance	11,400	15,600	12,000	9,000	48,000
Administration	22,800	31,200	24,000	18,000	96,000
Profit/(loss)	52,600	168,700	(48,000)	153,000	326,300

Annex 2

QUESTKING LTD

INTERNAL MEMO

To: Helen Johnson, Managing Director

From: Ann Fowler, Marketing Director

Date: 20 November

Subject: Future of Division C

I note from the budget for next year that Division C will, yet again, be reporting a loss. Given that the Board of Directors agreed at its last meeting to concentrate on improving the profitability of Questking Ltd, it is now time that we considered closing down Division C. If Division C were to be closed down, there would be an immediate increase in company profit of £197,600.

I think it would be a good idea to discuss the future of Division C at our next board meeting.

Annex 3

QUESTKING LTD
INTERNAL MEMO

To: Helen Johnson, Managing Director

From: Tony Anderson, Production Director

Date: 23 November

Subject: Fire at Modern Suppliers Ltd

You have probably read newspaper reports about the recent fire at Modern Suppliers Ltd. This has serious implications for Division B. Modern Suppliers are the sole manufacturers of the raw material used in all the products made by Division B. I have checked elsewhere and there is no acceptable substitute.

Yesterday, the sales director of Modern Suppliers Ltd wrote to me. Apparently, the factory which supplied us was totally destroyed and it will be at least a year before production recommences. He is, however, able to obtain limited supplies from their other factory. Unfortunately, the maximum they can supply to Division B is 26,800 kg over the next twelve months.

This means we will need to rearrange production. In summary, the original budget for next year showed a total output of 8,000 units which was to generate a profit of £326,300 for Division B. The individual product profitability and raw material usage was:

Product	P1	P2	P3	P4	Total
Units	1,900	2,600	2,000	1,500	8,000
Raw materials (kg)	7,600	13,000	8,000	12,000	40,600
Net profit/(loss)	£52,600	£168,700	(£48,000)	£153,000	326,300
Unit profit/(loss)	£27.68	£64.88	(£24)	£102.00	£40.79

As you can see, there is insufficient raw material to keep the original budget. Product P3 continues to make a loss and so I propose that we stop its manufacture. Given that the budgeted sales volumes are the maximum we can realistically sell, I suggest that the production schedule for next year should be determined by product profitability. The revised production schedule and divisional profitability will then be:

	Production units	Unit profit	Total profit	Material per unit	Material used	Material remaining
Material available						26,800 kg
Product P4	1,500	£102.00	£153,000	8 kg	12,000 kg	14,800 kg
Product P2	2,600	£64.88	£168,688	5 kg	13,000 kg	1,800 kg
Product P1	450	£27.68	£12,456	4 kg	1,800 kg	nil

I would be grateful if we could agree this proposal at the next board meeting.

MIDTOWN ENTERPRISE AGENCY

18 The Quadrant
Midtown Science Park
Midtown MX14 1YZ

25 November 20XX

Ms Helen Johnson
Managing Director
Questking Ltd
Mill Road
Midtown MX14 8XY

Dear Helen

Future Strategy of Division A

At the last board meeting, you asked me to make proposals for the future development of Division A. Division A makes modems enabling users of personal computers to connect to the Internet. Initially, Division A was a market leader but competitors have recently introduced faster modems. This accounts for the decreasing demand for the output of the division. Clearly, if this problem is not addressed then Division A will soon be no longer viable.

There are two options available to Questking Ltd. These are:

- Do nothing and close down the division when it becomes no longer profitable

- Develop a new modem

I have spoken to both Tony Anderson, your production director, and the technical experts at the enterprise agency. If you choose to develop a new modem, this will involve considerable development time and could not be introduced for at least two years even if development work started immediately. By then, Division A may have become a drain on the resources of Questking Ltd.

Given your wish to remain in the modem market, the first option is not recommended. It is possible, however, to improve the profitability of Division A's existing operations until the new modem is ready to be marketed.

I have been looking at Division A's costs. The factory employees are paid a relatively low basic wage which is then supplemented by a piecework payment for every modem produced. Sales staff are also paid a relatively low salary plus a commission of 5% on selling price. My proposal involves paying both groups a higher basic remuneration but lower commissions and piecework payments.

I have discussed this with John Peters, your company secretary, who showed me Division A's budget for the first quarter of next year. My proposals are to:

- Pay production workers a total of £280,000 per year as basic wages plus £3 for each modem produced.

- Pay sales staff an additional salary but to reduce their commission to 2%. The effect of this would be to increase selling expenses to £100,000 per year to reduce the amount paid as sales commission.

Reproduced below is Division A's proposed budget for the first quarter and the budget as it would appear if my proposals are accepted.

Division A budget for quarter 1	*Original budget*	*Revised budget*
Units produced and sold	9,000	9,000
	£	£
Turnover	450,000	450,000
Material	198,000	198,000
Labour[1]	97,500	97,000
Fixed production overhead absorbed	36,000	36,000
Gross profit	118,500	119,000
Sales commission[2]	22,500	9,000
Fixed production overhead unabsorbed	4,000	4,000
Selling expenses[3]	15,000	25,000
Central overheads:		
Personnel	8,500	8,500
Finance	4,500	4,500
Administration	5,500	5,500
Net profit	58,500	62,500

1	Labour:		
	Wages per quarter £280,000/4		£70,000
	Piecework 9,000 modems × £3		£27,000
	Total		£97,000
2	Sales commission £450,000 × 2%		£9,000
3	Selling expenses £100,000/4		£25,000

I would suggest that this proposal is added to the agenda for the next meeting of the board of directors.

Yours sincerely

Neil Henderson

Neil Henderson
Counsellor

QUESTKING LTD
INTERNAL MEMO

To: Helen Johnson, Managing Director

From: Ann Fowler, Marketing Director

Date: 26 November

Subject: Special order from Past Computers Ltd

I have recently been having discussions with the directors of Past Computers Ltd. Past Computers Ltd sell computers and software as a total package to the general public through newspaper advertisements. They are prepared to purchase 12,000 of the current modems manufactured by Division A if we can guarantee delivery of that number over the next twelve months and make a small modification to the modem. The modification involves the adding of an additional printed circuit. Past Computers feels there is a demand for the modified modems if they are already installed in the computers as part of the all-inclusive price.

Past Computers are prepared to purchase the 12,000 modified modems for £44 each. I know this is less than our price for next year but there will be some savings in costs. Because this is a centrally negotiated order, there will be no sales commission payable. In addition, we will not have to use our normal packaging and this will reduce the cost of materials of £1 per modem.

Even with these savings, however, it looks as though the contract will make a loss. Looking at Division A's budget for next year, revenue is planned to be £1.5 million, sales volume 30,000 and profit £114,000. This makes the unit selling price £50.00 and unit profit £3.80. The £6.00 reduction in selling price is greater than the unit profit and so the loss per unit will be £2.20 before paying for the cost of the modification.

Although there will be no additional cost of labour for the modification, there is the cost of the additional printed circuit. These currently cost £18.00 each. Fortunately we have 9,000 of the printed circuits in stock which were used on last year's model and have no further use other than being sold for scrap for £36,000. According to the stock records, these 9,000 items cost £16 each - a saving of £2 compared with buying from the manufacturer.

If the cost of making the modems ourselves involves too great a loss, there is one other option. We could sub-contract the work to Bright Processors Ltd. We have used them in the past when we had insufficient capacity to meet demand and we found them extremely reliable. I have spoken to their sales manager who tells me they would be prepared to make the modified modem for £46 providing we gave them a minimum order of 1,000 modified modems. Although this would result in a loss of £24,000 on the contract, that appears less than making the modified modem ourselves.

As you are aware, I have been trying to sell to Past Computers for several years and this is the first time they have been prepared to place an order. It might, therefore, be worthwhile accepting the order as a loss-leader in order to establish a basis for future custom.

Annex 6

QUESTKING LTD

INTERNAL MEMO

To: Helen Johnson, Managing Director

From: John Peters, Company Secretary

Date: 27 November

Subject: Possible contact with Meldreth plc

Since preparing the budget for Division D, an opportunity has arisen to bid for a four year contract to provide Meldreth plc with timers. A copy of their terms is enclosed with this memo. If we gain the contract, it will be necessary to purchase a machine costing £480,000. Division D has a machine which is no longer suitable for its needs. This can be sold for £80,000. The machine will have no further use after four years and its realisable value will be negligible. The net investment is, therefore, only £400,000. The supplier can also deliver the machine in the second week of January, well before the date required to commence the contract although after our accounting year end of 31 December.

As Questking Ltd has no other assets on which it claims capital allowances, another advantage will be the tax saving from the writing down allowance given by the Inland Revenue of 25%. Corporation tax at 30% will then be payable at the end of the following year.

There will be no further finance required as Meldreth will pay for the timers on delivery and we will not keep any form of stock ourselves. As £400,000 is beyond the spending limit of the manager of Division D, I have carried out a financial appraisal.

You will notice that Meldreth plc requires us to reduce prices by 20% on the preceding year's price after the first year. Although this seems excessive, I am reliably informed by the manager of Division D that material costs will also fall at a similar rate over those years. Because the 20% reduction in selling price is matched by the 20% reduction in material prices, I have ignored both reductions in my appraisal. Labour cost per unit will be £20 in the first year although subsequent wages increases are likely to be a compound 3% per year. Again, I have ignored this as the amount is so small.

Unit profit: Selling price - year 1	£120
Materials - year 1	£60
Labour - year 1	£20
Reapportioned overheads - including depreciation	£20
Unit profit	£20
Yearly profit (£20 × 8,000 timers)	£160,000
Add 25% capital allowances (£480,000/4)	£120,000
	£280,000
Corporation tax at 30%	£84,000
Annual profit	£196,000

$$\text{Return on investment} = \frac{£196,000}{£400,000} = 49\%$$

As the return of 49% is greater than our required return of 25%, I recommend that we bid for the contract.

MELDRETH PLC

Midtown Industrial Estate, Midtown MX15 2MZ

Tel: 0199 984235

Invitation to Tender

The Company and its suppliers

Meldreth plc is a major provider of industrial washing machines. Our leading market position has arisen from a policy of continuous improvement and Total Quality Management. Approved suppliers must demonstrate a similar commitment.

Approved suppliers must agree to flexible deliveries in support of our Just in Time stock procedures. In exchange for this commitment, Meldreth plc undertakes to pay suppliers within 24 hours of delivery.

The contract

The contract is for four years and involves supplying the company with 8,000 timers in each of those years. For the purpose of this contract, the year will be from 1 January to 31 December and deliveries in the first year are to commence from 1 February.

The price paid per timer in the first year will be £120.00. Efficiency gains are to be expected in subsequent years and so the company will only pay 80% of the previous year's price in the subsequent 3 years.

Suppliers wishing to bid for this contract should notify Meldreth plc by 1 January.

Extract from Questking's accounting procedures manual

2.1 Budget assumptions

- In preparing division budgets for the forthcoming year, divisional accountants should identify all assumptions concerning trends and provide explanations in writing for any increase or decrease in sales volumes compared with the current year.

- Divisions should assume no change in stocks, enabling production and sales to be the same.

- Divisions should plan for no change in selling prices or input costs during the year.

2.2 Developing the divisional budget

- Budgets should use the standard layout reproduced below to assist future consolidation.

- Material and labour should be treated as varying with production and sales volume except in the case of Division A where there is a fixed element to the labour cost. Sales commission is to be payable as a percentage of selling price and not units sold.

- All other expenses are to be treated as fixed costs.

- Budgets should be prepared for each quarter of the forthcoming year if sales and production levels vary between quarters. If sales and production are constant throughout the year, a single, annual budgeted profit statement is sufficient.

- Where divisions make more than one product, a budgeted profit statement should be prepared for each product.

2.3 Fixed overheads

- Fixed production overhead is to comprise the following: light, heat and power; rent; and rates. These should be absorbed on the basis of *maximum* possible volume. Division A should use the actual costs incurred last year, adjusted for any known or likely changes. Divisions B, C and D will have fixed production overhead apportioned to them on the basis of floor area.

- Selling expenses comprise the salaries of sales staff employed by each division plus all other selling and marketing expenses unique to the division. Company-wide selling and marketing expenses will be recharged to divisions through the central administration charge.

- Central fixed overheads comprise the costs of personnel, finance and administration. These are appointed to all divisions using a formula which takes account of the number of staff, the number of purchase invoices, the number of sales invoices and technical estimates.

- It has not proven possible to calculate depreciation for each division due to divisions making use of each others' plant, machinery and equipment. A company-wide depreciation charge of £80,000 has been calculated for the current year. This will be charged to divisions as part of the apportioned administration charge.

2.4 Pro forma budgeted profit statement for next year

- Turnover
- Material
- Labour

- Light, heat and power
- Rent
- Rates
- Sales commission
- Selling expenses
- Personnel
- Finance
- Administration
- Profit

3   Account year-end

The accounting year-end for Questking Ltd is 31 December.

4   Capital investments

- All capital expenditure above £20,000 must be approved by the board of directors.

- All investments should be evaluated using net present value techniques discounted at the company's cost of capital of 25%.

- Three digit discount tables, reproduced below, should be used in determining net present values.

- Any initial capital outlay should be shown as taking place at the beginning of the first year.

- Operating cashflows should be treated as occurring at the year-end.

- The nine month delay in paying any corporation tax should be treated as a one year delay for investment purposes.

Discount rate end of year	10%	15%	20%	25%	30%	35%
1	0.909	0.870	0.833	0.800	0.769	0.741
2	0.826	0.756	0.694	0.640	0.592	0.549
3	0.751	0.658	0.579	0.512	0.455	0.406
4	0.683	0.572	0.482	0.410	0.350	0.301
5	0.621	0.497	0.402	0.328	0.269	0.223
6	0.564	0.432	0.335	0.262	0.207	0.165
7	0.513	0.376	0.279	0.210	0.159	0.122
8	0.467	0.327	0.233	0.168	0.123	0.091
9	0.424	0.284	0.194	0.134	0.094	0.067
10	0.386	0.247	0.162	0.107	0.073	0.050

SUGGESTED FORMATS FOR ANSWERS

Task 1

Analysis of costs

	Division C budget £	Costs saved £	Costs not saved £
Turnover	2,240,000		
Material	789,000		
Labour	524,100		
Light, heat and power	150,000		
Rent	200,000		
Rates	300,000		
Sales commission	112,000		
Selling expenses	140,800		
Personnel	102,400		
Finance	76,800		
Administration	42,500		
Loss	(197,600)		

Task 2

Revised production schedule

	Production units	Material used kg	Material balance kg	Unit contribution £	Total contribution £
Material			26,800		
Product P1/P2/P3/P4					
Product P1/P2/P3/P4					
Product P1/P2/P3/P4					
Product P1/P2/P3/P4					
Revised contribution					———
Proposed contribution					
Increase in profit					———

Task 3

Calculation of existing fixed and variable costs of labour

	Quarter 1	Quarter 2	Quarter 3	Quarter 4
Units produced and sold	9,000	8,000	7,000	6,000
Labour (£)	97,500	92,000	86,500	81,000
Calculation:				

Task 5

MIDTOWN ENTERPRISE AGENCY

INVESTMENT PROPOSAL

Calculation of operating cashflows

End of year	Demand units a	Selling price b £	Cash received c $a \times b$ £	Material unit d £	Material total e $a \times d$ £	Labour unit f £	Labour total g $a \times f$ £	Net cash flow h $c - e - g$ £
1								
2								
3								
4								
5								
6								
7								
8								
9								

Note: complete as many years as there are operating cashflows.

Calculation of capital allowances

£

Capital cost
Writing down allowance - year 1 _____
Balance
Writing down allowance - year 2 _____
Balance
Writing down allowance - year 3 _____
Balance
Writing down allowance - year 4 _____
Balance
Writing down allowance - year 5 _____
Balance
Writing down allowance - year 6 _____
Balance
Writing down allowance - year 7 _____
Balance
Writing down allowance - year 8 _____
Balance
Writing down allowance - year 9 _____
Balance ═════════

Notes

Approved plant and machinery are entitled to a 25% writing down allowance. The number of years' allowances should equal the number of years' cashflows.

The final year's allowance is equal to the balance outstanding.

Calculation of taxable profit

End of year	Profit before depreciation £	Capital allowances £	Taxable profit £	Corporation tax @ 30% £	Payable in year
1					
2					
3					
4					
5					
6					
7					
8					
9					

Investment appraisal

End of year	Operating NCF £	Corporation tax £	Net cashflow £	Discount factors	Discounted cashflow £
1					
2					
3					
4					
5					
6					
7					
8					
9					

Present value of inflows   ————

Capital cost

Net present value   ————
                                         ════

Note: complete as many years as there are operating cashflows.

Answers

Practice activities: answers

1   ROBERT MOTHERWELL

> *Tutorial note.* In this fairly long question, it is important to work through each section carefully, as figures calculated early on are used later.

(a)   The **variable costs per unit** for the garden seat if the components are bought out as at present can be compared with the variable costs for own manufacture of the components.

	Components bought out	Own manufacture
Variable costs per unit	£	£
Raw materials	2.00	4.00
Components	8.00	2.00
Labour	3.00	6.00
Production overheads	1.00	2.00
	14.00	14.00

These figures show that there is no cost difference overall between the two options. Robert might still consider switching to own manufacture in order to have more control over production. However, if the components are bought from reliable sources, continuing to buy them in will save effort, may avoid problems and will allow more flexibility in using the spare production capacity for other purposes.

(b)   The current **profit per unit** for each product is as follows.

	Seats	Swings
	£	£
Selling price	30.00	40.00
Less commission (20%)	(6.00)	(8.00)
	24.00	32.00
Variable costs	(14.00)	(21.00)
Contribution	10.00	11.00
Fixed costs	(4.00)	(4.00)
	6.00	7.00

Total profit = (£6 × 2,000) + (£7 × 2,000) = £26,000

The profit if Robert does the marketing can be calculated as follows.

	£	£
Current profit		26,000
Commission saved		
£6 × 2,000	12,000	
£8 × 2,000	16,000	
		28,000
Additional costs	5,000	
Per unit (£4 × 4,000)	16,000	
		(21,000)
		33,000

Robert would do better to carry out his own marketing, as profits will increase by £7,000.

(c)   *Note*

To: Robert
From: A Technician

Buying a new machine will increase production of both swings and seats. There are a number of ways of evaluating whether the investigation is worthwhile.

The **payback period method** involves working out how quickly the investment 'pays for itself' in costs saved and extra revenue earned. The **average rate of return method** involves averaging accounting profits generated over future periods.

Less arbitrary than these two methods is the **net present value (NPV) method**, which takes into account the time value of money. The NPV method involves summing all cash flows arising from the investment, adjusted or 'discounted' to reflect the time value of money. The costs to be taken into consideration are 'relevant' costs only, as opposed to past 'sunk' costs which have already been incurred and therefore are irrelevant to current decision making. Depreciation on the existing machinery reflects 'sunk' costs and is therefore not relevant to the decision whether to buy the new machine.

(d)   Labour is a **limiting factor** for the purposes of this proposal.

Labour costs per units are £3 for the seats compared with £9 for the swing.

	Seats £	Swings £
Contribution per unit (see Task 2)	10.00	11.00
Labour cost per unit	3.00	9.00
Contribution per £1 of labour costs	3.33	1.22
Priority for manufacture	1st	2nd

Seats should be marketed more strongly, as the **contribution** per £1 of labour costs is higher than for swings. Production levels for the swings should be reduced.

The contribution for a swing is higher than for a seat. If production is limited to 6000 units and labour costs to £24,000, we should aim to market a combination of seats and swings with as many swings as possible given the limit on total labour costs.

If x = the number of seats
and y = the number of swings

Then	x	+	y	=	6,000	(1)
and	$3x$	+	$9y$	=	24,000	(2) (Labour costs)
(2) ÷ 3:	x	+	$3y$	=	8,000	(3)
(3) − (1):			$2y$	=	2,000	
			y	=	1,000	
and, from (1):			x	=	5,000	

Profits will be **maximised** if 1,000 swings and 5,000 seats can be sold.

2   JZ COMPANY

> *Tutorial note.* Since actual production was as budgeted for both months there will be no need to adjust for under- or over- absorbed fixed overhead when preparing the absorption costing statements. Part (c) of this question is a make or buy decision. The question specifically asks you to state any assumptions but you should get into the habit of doing this anyway, even if the task set does not prompt you to do so.

(a) (i)   Unit variable cost = £(4.50 + 1.50) = £6

Profit statements using marginal costing

	Month 1		Month 2	
	£'000	£'000	£'000	£'000
Sales		270		330
Variable cost of goods sold:				
Opening stock	-		12	
Production costs (20,000 × £6)	120		120	
	120		132	
Closing stock (2,000 × £6)	12		-	
		108		132
Contribution		162		198
Fixed overhead (20,000 × £3)		60		60
Profit		102		138

(ii)   *Profit statements using absorption costing*

	Month 1		Month 2	
	£'000	£'000	£'000	£'000
Sales		270		330
Cost of goods sold:				
Opening stock	-		18	
Production costs (20,000 × £9)	180		180	
	180		198	
Closing stock (2,000 × £9)	18		-	
		162		198
Profit		108		132

(b) As shown in the profit statements, the **stock valuation** is as follows.

Stock valuation at end of month 1

	£'000
Marginal costing, 2,000 units × £6	12
Absorption costing, 2,000 units × £9	18

(c) (i)

	£ per unit
Relevant cost of internal manufacture	
Direct material	1.20
Direct labour	2.25
Total relevant cost	3.45
External purchase price	3.65
Benefit of internal manufacture	0.20
Annual benefit of manufacturing (× 40,000)	£8,000

Assumptions

1   General fixed overhead cost will remain unaltered if the components are purchased externally.

2   Direct labour and material costs will be saved if the components are purchased externally.

(ii)

> *Tutorial note.* The question asks for one point to be considered but we have listed several so that you can see the type of factors that may be relevant.

Factors to be considered before finalising a decision are as follows.

(1) Is there any alternative use for the capacity, ie is there an **opportunity cost** involved?

(2) Does the company wish to be flexible and maintain **control** over operations by manufacturing its own requirements?

(3) Is the **quality** of the external supplier's components consistent and sufficiently high for the company's requirements?

(4) Would the supplier be **reliable** with delivery times?

(d) (i) *Assumptions*

1 There is no change in the level of fixed costs between years 1 and 2.

2 There is no change in selling prices or in unit variable costs between years 1 and 2.

	Sales £'000	Profit £'000
Year 2	280	36
Year 1	220	21
∴ Incremental sales/contribution	60	15

Since there is no change in fixed costs, the incremental profit is the additional contribution generated by sales of £60,000.

$$\therefore \text{Contribution to sales ratio} = \frac{15}{60} = 25\%$$

In year 2, contribution = £280,000 × 25%	=	£70,000
Profit	=	£36,000
∴ Fixed costs	=	£34,000
To earn a profit of £42,000,		
Required contribution	=	fixed costs + £42,000
	=	£34,000 + £42,000
	=	£76,000
∴ Required sales	=	$\dfrac{£76,000}{0.25}$
	=	£304,000

(ii)

Contribution from sales of £188,000	=	25% × £188,000
	=	£47,000
Fixed costs	=	£34,000
∴ Profit	=	£13,000

3 JK COMPANY

(a) *Assumptions*

(i) November is a representative month which can be used for forecast projections.

(ii) Fixed costs will remain unaltered despite the change in output volume and product mix.

(iii) Other cost and revenue patterns remain similarly unaltered.

Profit statement for one month with proposed changes to product mix

Product	J £	L £	M £	Total £
Sales revenue	6,720	2,040	9,500	18,260
Variable costs	3,150	1,275	6,375	10,800
Contribution	3,570	765	3,125	7,460
Fixed costs				3,860
Profit				3,600

(b) On the basis of the profit statement in part (a) the Marketing Director's proposals should be accepted and product K should be discontinued. Monthly profit increases to £3,600. The extra **contribution** from the increase in sales of the other products is sufficient to compensate for the loss of the contribution currently being earned by product K.

4 DELMAR

> *Tutorial note.* Since the question asks for a chart from which contribution can be read, the variable cost line will be drawn instead of the fixed cost line which is drawn on a traditional breakeven chart. The contribution is the area between the sales revenue line and the variable cost line.

(a) *Data for 80,000 units*

	£
Sales revenue = 80,000 × £40 =	3,200,000
Variable cost = 80,000 × £28 =	2,240,000
Fixed cost = 80,000 × £4	320,000
Total cost for 80,000 units	2,560,000

See contribution chart below.

(b) **If unit wage costs** increase by 10%, the variable cost per unit will increase by £2.20 to £30.20.

Revised cost data for 80,000 units

	£
Variable cost (80,000 × £30.20)	2,416,000
Fixed cost	320,000
Total cost for 80,000 units	2,736,000

These adjustments are shown by dotted lines on the chart.

Delmar - Contribution chart

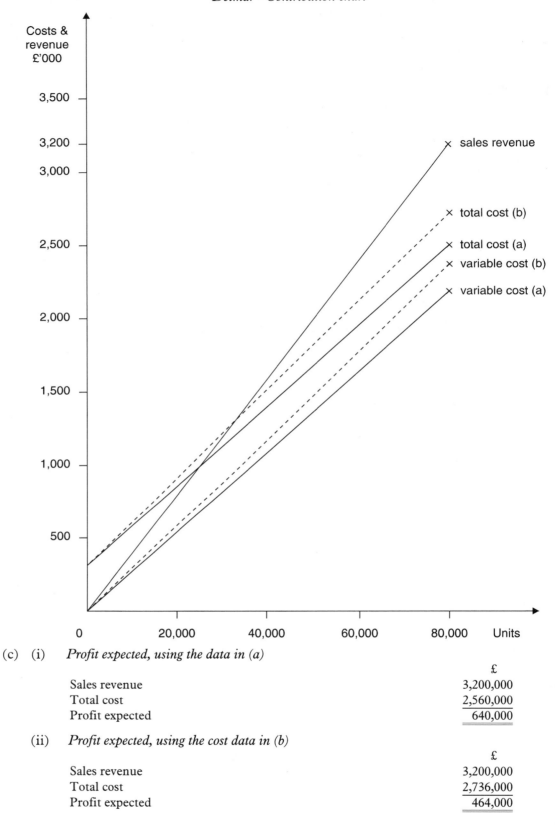

(c) (i)   *Profit expected, using the data in (a)*

		£
Sales revenue		3,200,000
Total cost		2,560,000
Profit expected		640,000

(ii)   *Profit expected, using the cost data in (b)*

		£
Sales revenue		3,200,000
Total cost		2,736,000
Profit expected		464,000

(d)   If the wage increase occurs, **contribution per unit** will be £(40 – 30.20) = £9.80 per unit

Contribution required	= current profit + fixed costs
	= £640,000 + £320,000
	= £960,000
∴ Volume required	= £960,000 ÷ £9.80 per unit
	= 97,959 units, to the nearest whole unit

(e)   The **assumptions** that are made when preparing breakeven charts are as follows.

(i)   There is a constant **selling price per unit**.

This assumption is necessary so that a straight line can be drawn to represent sales revenue. However this may not be valid because a lower price may be necessary to achieve higher sales volumes.

(ii)   The **variable cost per unit** is constant.

Again, this assumption is made so that a straight line can be drawn on the chart. It is unlikely that variable costs will remain constant for a wide range of activity. Changes which could occur include the following.

(1)   Material cost per unit may fall if discounts are available for bulk purchases.

(2)   Labour cost per unit may increase if it is necessary to pay bonus or overtime rates to achieve higher outputs.

(iii)   **Fixed costs** are constant.

Fixed costs are only likely to be constant within the 'relevant range'. Outside this range there could be steps in the total fixed cost, therefore a chart must not be used to predict the results for activities outside the relevant range.

(iv)   Where a chart is drawn for more than one product, the **mix of products** is constant.

This assumption is made so that the chart can be drawn based on the average sales revenue per unit and the average unit costs that will result from a constant mix of product. Since it is unlikely that the mix of products will remain constant in practice, this assumption severely limits the practical application of breakeven charts in a multi-product situation.

5   CINEMA CHAIN

> *Tutorial note.* The only fixed costs are the head office costs which have been apportioned to the cinemas on the basis of budgeted ticket receipts. These costs must be excluded from the overheads in order to determine the budgeted contribution.
>
> In part (e), receipts increase by 50%. The question explains that all costs are variable and therefore increased receipts, which implies an increase in cinema goers, will lead to an increase in variable costs. Obviously, in reality, if more people visit the cinema it is unlikely that film hire, wages and salaries and so on will increase proportionately but the information in the question leads you to calculate a 50% increase in contribution.

(a)   *Working*

	Reading £'000	*Newbury* £'000	*Basingstoke* £'000	*Total* £'000
Overheads	500	400	350	1,250
Apportioned head office costs	320	240	160	720
Variable overheads	180	160	190	530

(i)   *Marginal costing statement based on original budget*

	Reading		Newbury		Basingstoke		Total
	£'000	£'000	£'000	£'000	£'000	£'000	£'000
Ticket receipts		1,600		1,200		800	3,600
Variable costs							
Film hire	500		400		390		1,290
Wages and salaries	300		250		160		710
Variable overhead	180		160		190		530
		980		810		740	2,530
Contribution		620		390		60	1,070
Head office fixed costs							720
Profit							350

(ii)   *Marginal costing statement if the Basingstoke cinema is closed*

	Reading	Newbury	Total
	£'000	£'000	£'000
Ticket receipts	1,600	1,200	2,800
Variable costs	980	810	1,790
Contribution	620	390	1,010
Head office fixed costs			720
Profit			290

(b)   On the grounds of **profitability**, the Basingstoke cinema should not be closed, because it earns a **contribution** of £60,000. The overall profit for the cinema chain would fall by £60,000 because ticket revenue of £800,000 would be lost and variable costs of only £740,000 would be saved. The £160,000 of **head office fixed costs** apportioned to the Basingstoke cinema would still be incurred if it was closed down.

(c)

	Reading	Newbury	Basingstoke
Budgeted ticket receipts (£'000)	1,600	1,200	800
Number of tickets ('000) (÷ £4)	400	300	200
Contribution (£'000)	620	390	60
Contribution per ticket	£1.55	£1.30	£0.30

(d)   Breakeven point in revenue $= \dfrac{\text{fixed costs}}{\text{c / s ratio}}$

	Basingstoke open	Basingstoke closed
Contribution/sales ratio	1,070/3,600	1,010/2,800
	= 29.72%	= 36.07%
Breakeven point in revenue	720/0.2972	720/0.3607
	= £2,422,611	£1,996,119
Budgeted revenue	£3,600,000	£2,800,000
Margin of safety in revenue	£1,177,389	£803,881

(e)

Increase in contribution as a result of campaign	= 50% × present contribution
	= 50% × £60,000
	= £30,000
Cost of advertising campaign	£40,000
Reduction in profit	£(10,000)

The advertising campaign should not be undertaken because the extra contribution is less than the cost of the campaign. In addition the extra fixed cost will increase the breakeven point and will reduce the margin of safety.

6   SENSITIVE GAMES

Cost/revenue item	Basis of apportion- ment	Total £	Pool £	Bad- minton £	Indoor bowls £	Snack bar £	Admin- istration £
Snack bar provisions	(i)	4,750	-	-	-	4,750	-
Cleaning materials	(i)	5,000	5,000	-	-	-	-
General costs	(ii)	35,000	19,250	3,500	3,500	1,750	7,000
Employees pay	(iii)	100,000	25,000	5,000	5,000	5,000	60,000
Administration	(iv) (W1)	-	41,875	8,375	8,375	8,375	(67,000)
Snack bar revenue (i)		(40,000)				(40,000)	
Surplus on snack bar	(v) (W2)	-	(12,075)	(4,025)	(4,025)	20,125	
Net total cost		104,750	79,050	12,850	12,850		
Revenue		(50,000)	(30,000)	(10,000)	(10,000)		
Deficit		54,750	49,050	2,850	2,850		

Key

(i)   Allocation

(ii)   Area

(iii) £5,000 per employee

(iv)   Number of employees

(v)   Revenue

Workings

1

	Total	Pool	Badminton	Indoor bowls	Snack bar
Number of employees		8	5	1	1
Administration cost	£67,000	(5/8)£41,875	(1/8)£8,375	(1/8)£8,375	(1/8)£8,375

2

	Total	Pool	Badminton	Indoor bowls
Revenue (£'000)	50	30	10	10
Surplus on snack bar	£20,125	(30/50)£12,075	(10/50)£4,025	(10/50)£4,025

7   HOTEL

Tutorial note. The profit margin was 30% on *price*, not 30% on cost. To calculate the profit margin (£) on price use the following formula:

$$\text{Profit margin (£)} = \frac{\text{profit margin (\%)}}{100\% - \text{profit margin (\%)}} \times \text{cost (£)}$$

To calculate the profit margin (£) on cost use the following formula:

Profit margin (£) = profit margin (%) × cost (£)

(a) *Hotel cost statement*

	Accommodation £	Catering £	Leisure £	Outings £	Total £
Labour	110,000	100,500	35,000	38,500	284,000
Materials	19,000	36,000	16,000	13,000	84,000
Power (kilowatt hrs)	20,000	10,000	50,000	4,000	84,000
Rent and rates (floor area)	36,000	12,000	18,000	6,000	72,000
Depreciation (machinery value)	5,000	10,000	30,000	15,000	60,000
Advertising (customer usage)	30,000	24,000	16,000	6,000	76,000
	220,000	192,500	165,000	82,500	660,000
Office expenses (total cost)	80,000	70,000	60,000	30,000	240,000
Total cost	300,000	262,500	225,000	112,500	900,000
Number of customer days	15,000	12,000	8,000	3,000	
Cost per day	£20	£21.875	£28.125	£37.50	

(b)

	Cost per day per person £		Total cost for 1 person £
Accommodation	20.000	× 7 =	140.000
Catering	21.875	× 7 =	153.125
Leisure	28.125	× 3 =	84.375
Outings	37.500	× 3 =	112.500
			490.000
Profit (3/7 × £490)			210.000
Price per person			700.000
Price per couple for 1 week			£1,400.00

(c)

Cost centre		Costs absorbed £	Actual cost £	(Under)/over absorption £
Accommodation	£20.000 × 15,250	305,000	320,000	(15,000)
Catering	£21.875 × 13,000	284,375	275,000	9,375
Leisure	£28.125 × 6,800	191,250	200,000	(8,750)
Outings	£37.500 × 3,200	120,000	125,000	(5,000)

(d) There are two alternative methods that could be used to price food stuffs to the catering cost centre. They are **first in first out (FIFO)** and **last in first out (LIFO)**. Both methods would charge out the food on the basis of actual costs which is preferable to the present system whereby cost centres not actually involved in catering are charged with adverse variances.

The FIFO method assumes that food is charged out in the order in which it is purchased whereas the LIFO method assumes that food is charged in the reverse order to which it was purchased (in other words, on the basis of the most recent purchase first.) The LIFO method would meet the hotel manager's requirements as food would be charged to the catering department at its most current price, thereby taking account of the rapid movement of food prices.

8 PRODUCT OMEGA

Tutorial note. even if another absorption method had been used (see (a)) the overhead cost/unit would still have been £5 per unit, so the basis used would be irrelevant.

(a) The firm only makes one product so it is fair to split overheads equally among all units made, ie use a **units basis** for absorption.

(b) (i) **Fixed production overhead absorption rate** $= \dfrac{£4,500}{900} = £5$ per unit

Profit statements using absorption costing

	September		October	
	£	£	£	£
Sales revenue (W1)		18,000		34,500
Cost of goods sold:				
Opening stock	-		1,950	
Direct cost (W2)	6,000		8,000	
Fixed production overhead				
absorbed (W3)	3,750		5,000	
	10,500		14,450	
Less closing stock (W5)	(1,950)		-	
Under/(over) absorbed				
fixed o/h (W4)	750		(500)	
		(8,550)		(14,450)
Profit		9,450		20,050

(W1) Sales:
September $= 600 \times £30$
October $= 1,150 \times £30$

(W2) Direct costs:
September $= 750 \times £8$
October $= 1,000 \times £8$

(W3) Fixed production overhead:
September $= 750 \times £5$
October $= 1,000 \times £5$

(W4) Under/(over) absorption:
September $= £4,500 - £3,750$
October $= £4,500 - £5,000$

(W5) Closing stock:
September $= 150$ units $\times £(8 + 5)$

(ii) *Profit statements using marginal costing*

	September		October	
	£	£	£	£
Sales revenue		18,000		34,500
Variable cost of goods sold:				
Opening stock	-		1,200	
Direct costs	6,000		8,000	
	6,000		9,200	
Less closing stock ($150 \times £8$)	(1,200)		-	
		4,800		9,200
Contribution		13,200		25,300
Fixed production overhead		(4,500)		(4,500)
Profit		8,700		20,800

(c)

	September	October
	£	£
Absorption costing profit	9,450	20,050
Less: fixed overhead c/f in closing stock($150 \times £5$)	(750)	-
Add: fixed overhead b/f in opening stock $150 \times £5$)	-	750
Marginal costing profit	8,700	20,800

9 DELTA MANUFACTURING

To: The Chairman, Delta Manufacturing
From: AN Accountant
Date: 10 January 20X0

Evaluation of proposals to meet a profit target of £40,000

I have set out below a brief financial evaluation of the proposals set out by the board members.

Proposal (1)

Contribution needs to be £240,000 (fixed costs £200,000 plus target profit £40,000). This proposal will increase variable costs per unit by £5.00.

Therefore the contribution per unit is:

(a) Up to 12,000 = £70 (W1) - £55 = £15
(b) Over 12,000 = £70 (W1) - £65 = £5

The first 12,000 sales will give a contribution of £180,000 (ie 12,000 × £15).

The balance of £60,000 (240,000 – 180,000) at £5 per unit means additional sales of 12,000 (60,000/5) units to achieve target profit, ie 24,000 in all.

Conclusion

An increase in sales of 15,000 units (24,000-9,000) will be required. This represents an increase of 166.7%.

Proposal (2)

This proposal will increase the planned contribution to £260,000 by the increase of £20,000 in fixed costs.

Contribution per unit:

(a) Up to 12,000 = £70 – £50 = £20
(b) Over 12,000 = £70 – £60 = £10

(a) Contribution of first 12,000 units = £20 × 12,000 = 240,000
(b) Balance = £(260,000 – 240,000) = 20,000.
At £10 per unit this is 2,000 units.

Conclusion

An increase in sales of 5,000 is required to achieve the target profit. This represents an increase of 55.55%.

Proposal (3)

This proposal results in the contribution per unit dropping by £5 at all levels. This is equivalent in effect to increasing variable costs by the same amount. As this is exactly the same as the suggestion in (a) the consequences are the same, ie an increase in sales of 166.7% will be required.

Proposal (4)

This proposal will decrease the variable cost by £10 per unit. The more modern machinery will, however, give the company higher fixed costs.

Contribution per unit (at 9,000) = £70 – £40 = £30

	£
Total contribution = £30 × 9,000 =	270,000
Contribution required	240,000
Available for fixed costs	30,000

Conclusion

Fixed machine costs of up to £30,000 per period can be incurred before they affect the required profit.

Workings

(1) Selling price
     December 20X2

	£
Variable costs 9,000 × £50 =	450,000
Fixed costs	200,000
	650,000
Loss	20,000
Sales	630,000

$$\text{Selling price} = \frac{£630,000}{9,000} = £70$$

10   SMALL CONTRACTOR

> *Tutorial note.* Even though not asked for in the task, note the 'other factors' that should be considered in part (a).

(a) *Revised cost estimate, calculated on opportunity cost basis*

Relevant cost flows	£
Material X (note 2)	(20,000)
Material Y (note 3)	(13,000)
Direct material (actual purchase cost)	(12,000)
Skilled staff (variable overheads) (note 4)	(4,960)
Extra skilled worker (note 5)	(1,080)
Trainees (variable overhead (note 6)	(1,000)
Lost rental on curing press (note 7)	(2,000)
Subcontract work	(20,000)
Supervisory staff - overtime (note 8)	(1,000)
Relevant cost of contract	(75,040)

Based on the above figures, there is justification for the proposition that the contractor should tender for the contract, quoting less than £100,000.

However, particularly since the job is larger than he would normally consider, there are **other factors** which should be considered. Will the contract cause cash flow problems? Would a movement in interest rates affect the contractor's decision to tender?

Note 1: The £2,500 already spend by the estimating and design department is a sunk cost and can therefore be ignored.

Note 2: If the material X is not used in the contract is can be sold for £20,000, therefore if the contract is undertaken there will be lost revenue of £20,000.

Note 3: Historic cost is sunk. Since the material is used regularly the material will be bought in for the project at a future cost of £130 × 100 units = £13,000.

Note 4: For labour half the cost relates to wage costs, half to overheads. It is assumed that salaries for existing workers are a fixed cost. However, the variable overhead will be an additional cost if they work.

	£
Skilled workers	13,600
Less extra worker (£100 × 12 weeks)	1,200
	12,400

Variable overheads £12,400 × ½ × 80% = 4,960

Note 5: The extra temporary worker is an extra cost apart from the fixed overheads included in his salary. Cost is:

	£
Wages (£1,200 × ½)	600
Variable overheads (£1,200 × ½ × 80%)	480
	1,080

Note 6: As for skilled workers it is assumed that the labour rate is a fixed cost. Therefore only the additional variable overheads need to be considered.

£2,500 × ½ × 80% = £1,000

Note 7: Since 1 month's depreciation is being charged, it is assumed that the curing press is being used for 4 weeks.

Therefore lost rental 4 × £500 = £2,000

Depreciation is not a cash flow and can therefore be ignored.

Note 8: Since no additional supervisory staff will be employed, the current salary will be paid anyway. The £1,000 overtime however will be an additional cost.

Note 9: The fixed overheads are just an allocation and therefore will not be changed in the contract is undertaken.

(b) (i) *The use of opportunity cost in decision-making*

The word 'decision' implies a choice between one or more alternatives, so it follows that for each choice made, there is an **opportunity cost**. It is not always necessary in decision-making explicitly to calculate opportunity cost. In a situation where there are two or more discrete alternative uses for a set of resources, then the most attractive use can be chosen, without recourse to opportunity cost calculations.

It is when the same set of resources are necessary inputs to more than one project, but scarcity precludes their being used in both projects, that an opportunity cost calculation becomes necessary. For example, if there are constraints on labour time for the manufacture of two products, management will need to identify the contribution/incremental profit forgone by utilising labour hours on one project as opposed to the other, this determining the most profitable use of this resource.

(ii) *The use of opportunity cost in cost control*

The technique of opportunity cost calculation is not really applicable to cost control, owing to its somewhat theoretical nature. Once a decision has been made, opportunity costs generally cease to be relevant. Typical budgetary and cost control systems use the **analysis of variances** as the principal means of cost control, and it is difficult to see how such means can be reconciled with the usage of opportunity cost calculations.

11   MR BELLE

(a)   (i)   Examples of an **opportunity cost** are the rental of £400 and his salary of £1,000. Both represent 'benefits foregone' if he decides to proceed with the new cassette.

(ii)   Examples of **sunk costs** are the £2,000 he has been charged for the report and the £3,000 development costs.

(b)   *Statement of relevant costs*

	SP=£10	SP=£9
	£	£
Expected revenue : 8,750 @ £10	87,500	
15,000 @ £9		135,000
Variable costs : 8,750 @ £8.25	(72,187)	
15,000 @ £7.75		(116,250)
Expected contribution	15,313	18,750
Fixed production costs	(12,125)	(16,125)
Opportunity costs - rental	(400)	(400)
- salary	(1,000)	(1,000)
Excess of expected relevant benefits over costs	1,788	1,225

Based on expected volumes, Mr Belle should accept the contract and set the **selling price** at £10 per cassette.

Further analysis based on maximum and minimum possible volume:

	(£10)	(£9)
	£	£
(i) *Maximum volumes*		
10,000 @ (£10 – £8.25)	17,500	
18,000 @ (£9 – £7.75)		22,500
Other costs (fixed)	13,525	17,525
Net benefit	3,975	4,975
	£	£
(ii) *Minimum volumes*		
7,500 @ £1.75	13,125	
12,000 @ £1.25		15,000
Other costs	13,525	17,525
Net benefit	(400)	(2,525)

(iii)   *Break-even volumes*
Production

Units	Up to 10,000 units	Above 10,000 units
	$\dfrac{3,525}{1.75}$	$\dfrac{17,525}{1.25}$
	= 7,729 units	14,020 units

(iv)   *Summary of profit*

	Maximum	Expected	Minimum
	£	£	£
Select price = £10	3,975	1,788	(400)
Select price = £9	4,975	1,225	(2,525)
Reject	-	-	-
Decision	SP = £9	SP = £10	Reject

The summary shows the range of volume over which each action should be taken. Based on expected volumes (assuming a symmetrical probability distribution) the project should be accepted with a selling price of £10.

The higher selling price could be considered safer, as the degree of dispersion of potential profits/loss about the expected value is less. Then if the minimum volumes prevailed, the loss would be minimised.

However the lower selling could be considered safer to the extent that expected volume (8,750 units) is well above the break-even level of sales, whereas with the higher selling price break-even is just below expected.

Further points to consider before the contract is accepted.

(1) How reliable are the sales estimates?

(2) Is the finance available for the contract?

(3) Does this contract affect Mr Belle's risk, and hence his required rate of return?

(4) Time scales: how long will this project be viable?

(5) Are there any other, more profitable, projects which have not been considered?

12 SHOE RETAILER

> *Tutorial note.* It is a good idea to state assumptions clearly.

(a) **Assumption:** The average cost per unit of £25 represents variable costs only.

$$\textbf{Breakeven point} = \frac{\text{Fixed costs}}{\text{Contribution per unit}} = \frac{£(90,000 + 150,000)}{£(40 - 25)}$$

$$= 16,000 \text{ pairs of shoes}$$

Margin of safety = Forecast sales – breakeven point

= 24,000 – 16,000 = 8,000 pairs of shoes, or 33.3% of forecast

(b)

Breakeven graph for sale of shoes

Working for graph

Sales revenue for 24,000 pairs = 24,000 × £40 = £960,000.

	£
Fixed cost = £90,00 + £150,000 =	240,000
Variable costs 24,000 pairs × £25 =	600,000
Total cost for 24,000 pairs	840,000

(c) *Advantages of breakeven analysis*

(i) Graphical representation of cost and revenue data can be more easily understood by non-financial managers.

(ii) A breakeven model enables the determination of the profit or loss at any level of activity within the range for which the model is valid, and the contribution to sales ratio can indicate relative profitability for different products.

(iii) Highlighting the breakeven point and the margin of safety gives managers some indication of the level of risk involved, and as such is an aid to production and sales.

Limitations of breakeven analysis

(i) It is often difficult to analyse costs into fixed and variable elements.

(ii) The assumption that fixed costs are constant is not necessarily valid as fixed costs rise in a 'step' function once certain production levels are reached (eg fixed costs of new machinery to increase production).

(iii) The basic model treats variable costs per unit as constant, which is not always a valid assumption (for example, because of quantity discounts).

(iv) The analysis is only possible for a single product or a constant product mix.

13 BREAKEVEN CHARTS

> *Tutorial note.* Breakeven charts and P/V charts are quite easy, but only if you can remember what goes where. Don't just assume you would know if it came to it in an assessment: practise to make sure!

(a)

	Total £	Fixed £	Variable (3,500 units) £	Variable cost per unit £
Materials	280,000	-	280,000	80
Labour	300,000	125,000	175,000	50
Reduction overhead (30:70)	150,000	45,000	105,000	30
Selling and distribution overhead (50:50)	140,000	70,000	70,000	20
Administration overhead	60,000	60,000	-	-
	930,000	300,000	630,000	180
Selling price				300
Contribution per unit				120
Total contribution (3,500 units)				£420,000

(b)

	£
Contribution (per (a))	420,000
Fixed costs (per (a))	300,000
Profit	120,000

(c)

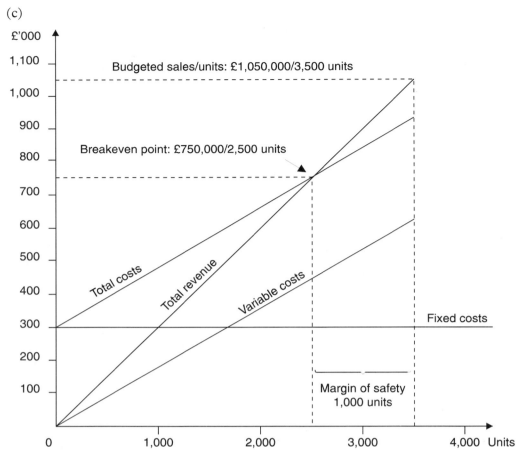

(d) **Breakeven analysis** (or CVP analysis) and charts are based on the following **assumptions.**

(i) Fixed costs are the same in total and variable costs are the same per unit at all levels of output.

(ii) The sales price is constant at all levels of activity.

(iii) There is no uncertainty in the estimation and categorisation of fixed and variable costs.

(iv) Production and sales are the same.

(e) The additional 500 computers will earn a contribution of £225 − £180 = £45 per computer towards fixed costs. In annual terms this means that profit will increase by £22,500. The offer is definitely worth accepting if it cannot be bettered and if it will not affect the price obtainable for the remaining 3,500 computers.

14   JETS LTD

> *Tutorial note.* The time allocations given reflect the number of marks allocated for each part when the paper was set in an AAT assessment.

(a) *Jets Ltd: proposed packing contract for Sykes Ltd*

Cost and profit statement for one week

Number of units to be packed and loaded = 200 per week

Variable costs	£ per unit	£	£
Packing materials	15.00	3,000	
Packing labour	0.80	160	
Loading labour	0.50	100	
Total variable cost	16.30		3,260
Fixed costs			
Packing labour	2.84	568	
Loading labour	1.75	350	
Hire of packing machine	0.50	100	
Administration and other costs	2.40	480	
Total fixed cost	7.49		1,498
Total cost	23.79		4,758
Sales value	27.00		5,400
Profit per week	3.21		642

(b)   (i)   Breakeven point $= \dfrac{£1,498}{£27 \; - \; £16.30} = 140$ units per week

     (ii)   Margin of safety $= (200 - 140)$ units $= 60$ units per week

                                                      $= 30\%$ of estimated activity

     (iii)

		£
Profit from 240 units =	contribution $(£27 - £16.30) \times 240$	2,568
	less fixed costs	1,498
	Weekly profit	1,070

(c)

JETS LIMITED

MEMORANDUM

To: Managing Director
From: Assistant Management Accountant
Date: 12 May 20X6
Subject: Proposed Sykes packing contract

(i)   *The forecast results for the contract*

The proposed contract will earn a profit of £642 per week at the estimated activity level of 200 units per week.

The breakeven point is 140 units per week and the margin of safety is 60 units per week. This indicates that if activity levels fall by more than 30% of projected activity then losses will be incurred on the contract.

If activity levels increase by 20% to 240 units per week then profit will increase by 67% to £1,070 per week. It would therefore be very beneficial to seek increases in activity levels, assuming that they can be accommodated within the current facilities.

(ii)   The problem with using the data supplied to forecast the profit result for 240 units is that this activity level is beyond the 'relevant range' for the data provided.

The calculations have assumed that the stated cost behaviour patterns apply for increased activity levels. This may not be the case, for example there may be a step in the fixed costs: more direct labour may be needed or supervisory costs may increase. Or perhaps it might be necessary to pay higher bonuses to achieve higher activity levels, which would change the variable cost per unit.

If forecasts are based on data which is collected for different activity levels, then management must be aware of its potential inaccuracies.

15 SECURITY SERVICES

> *Tutorial note.* The calculations for task (a) are quite short. Note that here we are effectively answering the question: how many hours of sales per month are required for the fixed costs to be covered by the contribution per hour?

(a) *Breakeven point*

Present situation $\dfrac{£18,000}{£(30-22)} = 2,250$ hours

Proposed situation $\dfrac{£39,000}{£(33-20)} = 3,000$ hours

(b) *Monthly profit*

Present situation:

Sales	=	5,200 hours
Breakeven	=	2,250 hours
Margin of safety	=	2,950 hours × £8 per hour contribution
Monthly profit		£23,600

Proposed situation:

Sales	=	5,200 hours
Breakeven	=	3,000 hours
Margin of safety	=	2,200 hours × £13 per hour contribution
Monthly profit		£28,600

(c) The changes will result in higher **fixed costs** and a higher **contribution per hour**. This means that if sales increase, then profits will grow more quickly because more contribution is earned per hour.

However it also means that **profits** will reduce more rapidly if sales start to fall in the future. This is reflected by the **higher breakeven point** and means that the proposed situation is more risky than at present.

16 SINGLE PRODUCT

> *Tutorial note.* For the purposes of this practice question, only an outline of the graph's axes has been given. Graph paper will be provided, if called for, in the 'live' assessments.

(a)

Per month at maximum production level	£
Sales (£17 per unit)	170,000
Variable costs ((£4 + £6) per unit)	100,000
Contribution ((£17 − £10) per unit)	70,000
Fixed costs	40,000
Profit	30,000

The lines for total costs and for sales at the maximum production level can be drawn on the graph using the information above, given that total costs are £40,000 when production is nil.

Reading off from the chart **on the next page**, the breakeven production level is approximately 5,700 units.

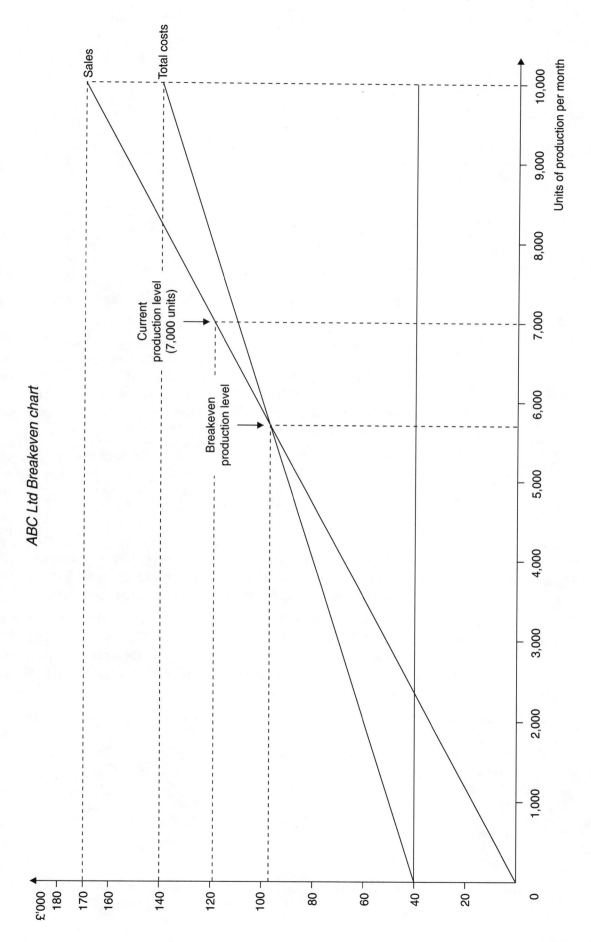

ABC Ltd Breakeven chart

(b) (i) Breakeven point $= \dfrac{\text{Total fixed costs}}{\text{Contribution per unit}} = \dfrac{40,000}{7} = 5,714$ units per month

The breakeven point thus occurs at a monthly production level of 5,714 units, as proved below.

	£
Sales (£17 × 5,714)	97,138
Variable costs (£10 × 5,714)	57,140
Contribution	39,998
Fixed costs	40,000
Small difference due to rounding	2

(ii)

Per month at current production level	£
Sales (£17 × 7,000)	119,000
Variable costs (£10 × 7,000)	70,000
Contribution	49,000
Fixed costs	40,000
Profit	9,000

At the current production level of 7,000 units per month, the profit is £9,000 per month.

(c) (i) DEF Ltd has **fixed costs** which, at £6,000 per month, are 1.5 times the fixed costs of ABC Ltd. However, its variable costs are lower, at £5 per unit compared with £10 per unit for ABC Ltd. It is likely that DEF Ltd is using a more capital intensive method of production than ABC Ltd. More use of capital machinery would save on labour and materials costs but is likely to involve **higher fixed costs** such as depreciation and premises costs.

(ii) The **contribution per unit** for the two companies is compared below.

Per unit	ABC Ltd	DEF Ltd
	£	£
Selling price	17.00	17.00
Variable costs	10.00	5.00
Contribution	7.00	12.00

Each company breaks even when its fixed costs are covered by the contribution. As we have seen, this occurs at 5,714 units per month for ABC Ltd. For DEF Ltd, the **breakeven point** is at 60,000 ÷ 12 = 5,000 units per month.

Beyond the breakeven point, DEF Ltd adds £12 to profit for every additional unit produced while ABC Ltd adds only £7 for every additional unit. Thus, DEF Ltd generates a higher rate of **profit per unit** beyond the breakeven point. This will be reflected on a breakeven graph for DEF Ltd by a flatter total costs line than for ABC Ltd.

(d) The profitability of ABC Ltd following the implementation of the proposed policy will be as follows.

Per month	£
Sales (£20 × 6,500)	130,000
Variable costs (£12 × 6,500)	(78,000)
	52,000
Fixed costs	42,000
Profit	10,000

17 BUILDING COMPANY

> *Tutorial note.* Don't forget headings, labels for axes, labels for lines, neatness and accuracy. Make sure that your graph shows clearly all the requirements of the question.

(a) (i) First we need to calculate the **fixed costs** for the period using the **high-low method**.

	Units	Profit
		£'000
High - March	30	250
Low - June	16	40
	14	210

Variable cost per unit (£210,000/14)	£15,000

Taking March as an example:	£'000
Sales (30 × £30,000)	900
Profit	250
Total costs	650
Variable costs (30 × £15,000)	450
Fixed costs	200

Fixed costs for the six months = 6 × £200,000 = £1,200,000.

(ii) We now need to calculate the **breakeven point** as follows.

Per unit	£'000
Selling price	30
Variable cost	15
Contribution	15

Breakeven point is where total contribution = fixed costs. Breakeven point is therefore where £15,000N = £1,200,000, where N is the breakeven quantity of units.

N = £(1,200,000/15,000) = 80 units

Breakeven sales revenue = 80 × £30,000 = £2,400,000

Breakeven chart

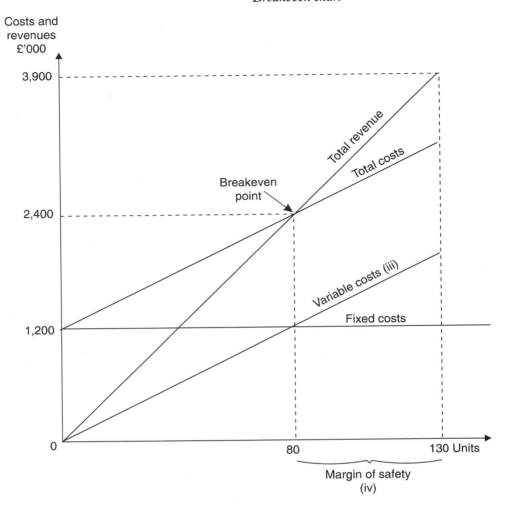

Note that at 80 units, the variable cost is 80 × £15,000 = £1,200,000.

(b)

	Present (130 units) Per unit £'000	Proposed (143 units) Per unit £'000
Selling price	30	25
Variable cost	15	15
Contribution	15	10
Total contribution	1,950	1,430
Fixed costs	1,200	1,200
Profit	750	230

The company should not reduce the **selling price** because, although extra units will be sold, contribution per unit will drop from £15,000 to £10,000 and total profit will drop by £520,000 (£(750,000 − 230,000)).

(c) It is an oversimplification to say that costs are readily identifiable as either fixed or variable throughout a range of production.

While many **variable costs** approximate to a **linear** behaviour pattern (rise in a straight line fashion as the volume of activity increases), some variable costs are in fact **curvilinear**, becoming either more expensive or cheaper per unit as activity levels change. A unit variable cost which might increase as activity increases is direct labour. Bonus payments might be paid progressively as certain levels of production are reached. An example of a variable cost becoming progressively cheaper per unit as activity increases is direct materials. **Discounts** are sometimes available when larger quantities are purchased.

Fixed costs do not necessarily remain fixed. While many fixed costs do remain constant within the relevant range of activity, there are likely to be steps or changes in the fixed cost if activity extends beyond this range. For example, it may be possible to operate with one salaried supervisor at a certain level of activity, but once this activity level is exceeded more supervisors are required and there is a resulting step in the fixed cost. This is known as **step cost behaviour**.

A lot of costs are actually **semi-fixed** (or semi-variable, or mixed). The increasing labour cost described above has a flat fixed rate and a variable bonus element and a telephone bill will have a fixed cost for rental and a variable cost depending on the number of calls made. Other cost patterns include step costs (supervisor, as described above, and rent, where accommodation requirements increase as output levels get higher) and patterns appropriate to certain items (such as where a bulk purchase discount applies retrospectively to all units purchased or where a discount applies only to units purchased in excess of a certain quantity).

18 ELECTRICITY

Relevant cost of contract

	Note	£
Material C	1	(2,000)
F	2	9,000
Operating labour	3	33,000
Supervisory labour	4	-
Cost of machinery	5	3,500
General overheads	6	-
Relevant cost		43,500
Revenue		70,000
Contribution from contract		26,500

On financial grounds the contract should be undertaken because it produces a **contribution** when reviewed on a **relevant cost basis**.

Notes

1   The original cost of material C is sunk and not relevant. Using material C on this contract saves the cost of disposal of £2,000.

2   The use of material F requires expenditure of £9,000 on buying material X, which would not otherwise be incurred. The original cost of material F is sunk.

3   The incremental cost incurred on labour as a result of this contract will be the cost of employing three new workers: 3 × £220 × 50 weeks = £33,000.

4   No extra cost will be incurred on supervisory labour. The £12,000 salary will be incurred anyway.

5   The original cost and depreciation of the machinery are sunk costs and not relevant. The relevant cost of using the machinery on this contract is:

	£
Scrap revenue forgone - opportunity cost	2,000
Disposal cost to be incurred in one year	1,500
	3,500

6   General overheads will not be affected by this contract. Therefore they are not relevant.

19 CONSULTANCY

The **opportunity cost** of the job would be as follows.

	£
Labour (30 hours × £45)	1,350
Computer time opportunity cost (5 hours × £50)	250
Supplies and expenses	200
	1,800

The opportunity cost of labour and computer time is the normal charge-out rate, of £45 and £50 per hour respectively.

A further addition to cost might be added for 'general overhead' depending on the system of costing being used.

The opportunity cost of the job shows that the firm would increase profits by accepting the job, by £(2,500 – 1,800) = £700.

20 KATRINA

(a)

Time	Flow	£	DF 10%	PV
0	Investment	(150,000)	1	(150,000)
1-5	Sales	250,000	3.791	947,750
1-5	Variable costs	(62,500)	3.791	(236,938)
1-5	Fixed costs	(50,000)	3.791	(189,550)
				371,262

Conclusion

The **NPV** is positive: therefore, accept this project.

(b) *Sensitivity*

All calculations are calculated as:

$$\frac{PV}{PV \text{ flow}} \times 100$$

(i) *Variable costs*

$$\frac{371,262}{236,938} \times 100 = \underline{156.7\%}$$

Variable costs would need to increase by 156.7% before the accept decision would change.

(ii) *Capital outlay*

$$\frac{371,262}{150,000} \times 100 = \underline{247.5\%}$$

The capital outlay would need to increase by 247.5% before the decision would change.

(iii) *Volume of sales*

Volume is represented by contribution.

$$\begin{aligned} \text{Contribution} &= \text{SP} - \text{VC} \\ &= £947,750 - £236,938 \\ &= £710,812 \end{aligned}$$

$$\therefore \frac{371,262}{710,812} \times 100 = \underline{52.2\%}$$

Volume would need to fall by 52.2% for the decision to change.

(iv) *Fixed costs*

$$\frac{371{,}262}{189{,}550} \times 100 = \underline{195.9\%}$$

Fixed costs would need to increase by 195.9% before the decision would change.

(c) (i) All the costs and revenues are assumed to be paid/received in arrears. In reality they will probably accrue evenly during the year.

(ii) All costs and revenues are estimates only.

(iii) It is assumed that the variable and fixed costs remain constant during the life of the project.

(iv) Inflation and taxation have been ignored.

(v) The costs of capital figure may not be accurate or appropriate for this project.

(vi) It is assumed that the objective of the company is to maximise shareholder wealth.

(vii) The project may affect the sales of other products. This has been ignored.

(viii) The company may not have the cash to buy the machine outright. Alternative forms of purchase, eg lease should be considered.

(ix) Sensitivity analysis changes only one variable at a time. This is unrealistic. A scenario based approach may be more appropriate such as simulation.

(x) Katrina Limited must consider how accurate the market research is.

(xi) The life of the project should be reviewed further - sales may exist beyond the five years.

21   STAPLES LTD

The **index number** for each year with 20X6 as the **base year** will be the original index number divided by 1.14, and the real wages for each year will be (money wages × 100) / index number for the year.

Year	Index	Real wage £
20X0	88	170
20X1	90	179
20X2	93	181
20X3	95	188
20X4	96	193
20X5	98	195
20X6	100	197
20X7	102	199
20X8	104	199
20X9	106	201
20Y0	108	214

22   INFLATION INDEX

Deflated value = $£X \times a/b$

23 SEASONAL VARIATIONS

	Spring	Summer	Autumn	Winter	Total
Year 1			+11.2	+23.5	
Year 2	−9.8	−28.1	+12.5	+23.7	
Year 3	−7.4	−26.3	+11.7		
Average variation	−8.6	−27.2	+11.8	+23.6	−0.4
Adjust total variation to nil	+0.1	+0.1	+0.1	+0.1	+0.4
Estimated seasonal variation	−8.5	−27.1	+11.9	+23.7	0.0

24 PROJECT APPRAISAL CALCULATIONS I

(a) and (b)

$$\text{Annual depreciation charge} = \frac{£75,000}{5} = £15,000$$

Adding back the depreciation charge, the cash flows for the project are as follows.

Year	Cash flow £	Discount factor	Present value £
0	(75,000)	1.000	(75,000)
1	55,000	0.870	47,850
2	45,000	0.756	34,020
3	25,000	0.658	16,450
4	5,000	0.572	2,860
5	5,000	0.497	2,485
		Net present value	28,665

Payback occurs at the point where cash flows in year 2 amount to £20,000.

∴ **Payback period** = 1 year + (20,000/45,000 × 1 year)

= 1½ years, approximately

(c) *Average accounting profit*

Year	£
1	40,000
2	30,000
3	10,000
4	(10,000)
5	(10,000)
	60,000

∴ Average accounting profit $= \dfrac{£60,000}{5} = £12,000$

Average investment $= \dfrac{\text{initial investment} + \text{scrap value}}{2}$

$= \dfrac{£75,000 + 0}{2} = £37,500$

∴ Accounting rate of return $= \dfrac{£12,000}{£37,500} \times 100\% = 32\%$

25 PROJECT APPRAISAL CALCULATIONS II

Depreciation is not a cash flow and is therefore excluded from the calculation of the payback period and the net present value.

Assumption: **General fixed overheads** are not affected by the decision to purchase the equipment and they are excluded from the calculations.

(a)   Annual contribution = 40,000 × £(4 – 2) = £80,000

Therefore, **payback period** = $\dfrac{£200,000}{£80,000}$ = 2.5 years, assuming even cash flows.

(b)   Sum of the discount factors for years 1 - 5   = 2.99

Present value of £80,000 contribution for 5 years   = 2.99 × £80,000

       = £239,200

Initial outlay   = £200,000

Therefore, **net present value** for the equipment   = £39,200

(c)   Increase in present value of the contribution = £239,200 × 10% = £23,920

Therefore, **percentage increase in net present value**   = $\dfrac{£23,920}{£39,200}$ × 100%

= 61%

26 FOUR PROJECTS

> *Tutorial note.* Poor answers when this question was set were mainly due to students' inability to define clearly the main investment appraisal methods, to differentiate between cash-based and profits-based methods and to emphasise the importance of the DCF method. The cost of capital was also little understood.

REPORT

To: The Board
From: Management Accountant
Date: 31 September 20X5
Subject: Investment appraisal

(a)   *Payback period*

This method of investment appraisal calculates the length of time a project will take to recoup the initial investment. In other words the report shows how long each project will take to pay for itself. The method is based on cashflows. On this basis project A should be chosen as it has the shortest payback period.

Accounting rate of return

This method calculates the profits that will be earned by a project and expresses this as a percentage of the capital invested in the project. One formula commonly used is

$$ARR = \frac{\text{Estimated average profit}}{\text{Estimated average invesment}}$$

The higher the rate of return, the higher a project is ranked and so project C is to be preferred on this basis.

Net present value

This method considers all relevant cash flows associated with a project over the whole of its life and adjusts those occurring in future years to 'present value' by discounting at a rate called the 'cost of capital', in this case 12%. The project to be chosen on this basis would be B because it has the highest net present value.

Internal rate of return

This method involves comparing the rate of return expected from the project calculated on a discounted cash flow (DCF) basis with the cost of capital. Projects with an IRR higher than the cost of capital are worth undertaking. In this case project B would be chosen.

(b) There are disadvantages to the use of the payback method and the accounting rate of return for investment appraisal. The payback method ignores any cashflows that occur after the project has paid for itself. Because of this a project that takes time to get off the ground but earns substantial profits once it is established might be rejected if the payback method is used.

The accounting rate of return is based on accounting profits rather than cash and it may therefore give too much emphasis to notional costs which are merely accounting conventions and not truly relevant to a project's performance. There are also differing views about the way in which ARR should be calculated.

Most importantly, both methods ignore the time value of money (£1 *now* can be re-invested *now* and so it is worth more than a promise of £1 in a year's time).

None of these objections apply to the NPV and IRR methods of investment appraisal and for this reason project B ought to be chosen as it has the highest NPV and the highest IRR.

(c) It is commonly held that the discount rate which a company should use as its cost of capital is one that reflects the rate of return expected by its investors: in this case by the investors in the 12% debentures. Debenture holders expect interest payments and a company must make enough profits from its own operations to pay interest.

Both the NPV and the IRR methods use the rate of 12% as the cost of capital as explained in (a) above.

(d) One of the major components of risk is uncertainty about the future, and one way of minimising risk is to avoid relying on long-term forecasts. In the circumstances described it would therefore be preferable to invest in the project with the shortest payback period, that is, project A.

(e) If the company can invest in all four projects it should choose any that give a positive net present value and an IRR greater than the cost of capital. This means that all projects except D will be chosen. D makes a loss overall in DCF terms, and the funds could be invested elsewhere at 12% which is greater than the 11% return offered by project D.

27   LOAMSHIRE LIBRARY

> *Tutorial note.* If you are asked to prepare a report, always set your work out as a report, with appropriate headings.

REPORT

To: The County Librarian
From: A Technician
Date: 6 July 20X4
Subject: Computer systems upgrade

Introduction

Two alternative projects A and B are under examination, each having different initial outlays and different estimated savings over time. The two alternatives are evaluated below using discounted cash flow (DCF) techniques (the net present value method with a 10% discount rate), in accordance with the county's policy for project evaluation.

Use of DCF techniques

The county uses discounted cash flow techniques. There are a number of reasons for preferring DCF techniques.

The payback method of investment appraisal calculates the length of time a project will take to recoup the initial investment. In other words it shows how long a project will take to 'pay for itself'. The method is based on cashflows.

The net present value (NPV) is a DCF technique which considers all relevant cash flows associated with a project over the whole of its life and adjusts those occurring in future years to 'present value' by discounting at a rate reflecting the 'cost of capital', in this case 10%.

There are disadvantages to the use of the payback method for investment appraisal. The method ignores any cashflows that occur after the project has paid for itself. Because of this, a project that takes time to get off the ground but earns substantial profits once it is established might be rejected if the payback method is used.

The payback method also ignores the time value of money (£1 *now* can be re-invested *now* and so it is worth more than a promise of £1 in a year's time).

The NPV method, in contrast, takes all project cash flows into account and the adjustments make using the DCF technique reflect the time value of the cash flows. Consequently, the NPV method has been adopted by the county in preference to the 'payback' method.

DCF appraisal

It is assumed that the cash savings occurs at the end of each year.

	Cash flows		Discount	Discounted cash flows	
	Project A	Project B	factor	Project A	Project B
	£	£	10%	£	£
Initial outlay	(75,000)	(100,000)	1.0000	(75,000)	(100,000)
Annual cash savings					
Year 1	20,000	30,000	0.9091	18,182	27,273
Year 2	30,000	45,000	0.8264	24,792	37,188
Year 3	30,000	45,000	0.7513	22,539	33,809
Year 4	25,000	40,000	0.6830	17,075	27,320
Year 5	20,000	-	0.6209	12,418	-
				20,006	25,590

Recommendation

Project B is the preferable option since its net present value using a discount rate of 10% is significantly higher at £25,590 compared with £20,006 for Project A.

28   WASH ME

> *Tutorial note.* A good general rule in preparing reports is to put calculations in an Appendix at the end, leaving the body of the report for an explanation of the results and any recommendations.

REPORT

To: General Manager
From: Assistant Management Accountant
Date: 13 June 20X5
Subject: Proposal to purchase vehicle cleansing machine

The results of the investment appraisal

I have carried out an appraisal of this proposal using the net present value method and the payback method. The results of my calculations are shown in the Appendix.

The cash flows from the project are forecast to pay back the initial outlay in approximately 2.7 years, which is a long payback period for a project with a life of only four years.

BPP PUBLISHING

However, the project generates a positive net present value of £12,018. This means that the wealth of the company would be increased by this amount if the project is undertaken (ignoring risk and inflation).

Recommendation concerning the proposal

Since the proposal is forecast to result in a positive net present value, I recommend that it should be accepted.

If I can be of any further assistance in this matter please do not hesitate to contact me.

APPENDIX: APPRAISAL CALCULATIONS

The net present value of the cash flows from the project

Year	Initial purchase £	Operating costs £	Labour savings £	Other cont'n £	Total cash flow £	Discount factor	Present value £
0	(80,000)				(80,000)	1.0000	(80,000)
1		(8,000)	25,000	12,600	29,600	0.9091	26,909
2		(8,400)	25,000	12,600	29,200	0.8264	24,131
3		(8,820)	25,000	12,600	28,780	0.7513	21,622
4		(9,261)	25,000	12,600	28,339	0.6830	19,356
					Net present value		12,018

Payback period

Year	Cumulative cash flow £
0	(80,000)
1	(50,400)
2	(21,200)
3	7,580

Payback period = 2 years + (21,200/28,780) = 2.7 years approximately, assuming even cash flows.

29 INVESTMENT PROJECTS

> *Tutorial note.* This is a straightforward investment appraisal question, but remember that *cash* flows must be used for payback and net present value calculations. The profits in the question are shown after including depreciation, which is not a cash flow. You will therefore need to add back the depreciation to arrive at the correct cash flow figures.

(a) Annual depreciation charge $= \dfrac{£75,000}{5} = £15,000$

Adding back the depreciation charge, the cash flows for the project are as follows:

Year	Project 1 cash flow (a) £	Discount factor	Project 1 present value £	Project 2 cash flow (b) £	Discount factor	Project 2 present value £
0	(75,000)	1.000	(75,000)	(75,000)	1.000	(75,000)
1	45,000	0.869	39,105	40,000	0.869	34,760
2	45,000	0.756	34,020	30,000	0.756	22,680
3	35,000	0.657	22,995	35,000	0.657	22,995
4	5,000	0.571	2,855	35,000	0.571	19,985
5	5,000	0.497	2,485	-	0.497	-
		Net present value	26,460 (ii)		Net present value	25,420 (ii)

Payback period (i):

Project 1 - using column (a) in above workings
= 1 year + (30/45 × 1 year) = 1.7 years.

Project 2   - using column (b) in above workings
$$= 2 \text{ years} + (5/35 \times 1 \text{ year}) = 2.1 \text{ years}.$$

(b) *Payback*

Advantages

1   Simple to use.

2   Assists the cash flow of the organisation by selecting projects with earlier net cash inflows.

3   Reduces the risk involved in investment by relying more on short-term forecasts, which are likely to be more reliable.

Disadvantages

1   Does not quantify the true value of money.

2   Ignores the overall profitability of the project.

3   Ignores any cash flows beyond the payback period.

Net present value

Advantages

1   Quantifies the time value of money by giving more weight to earlier cash flows, and less weight to more distant flows.

2   All cash flows are taken into account, whenever they occur.

Disadvantage

It is difficult to determine the appropriate discount rate to be used in the calculations.

(c)   Project 1 is recommended for acceptance, since it has the highest **net present value** and the shortest **payback period**. However, management should be prepared for the possible detrimental effect on cash flows of the accounting losses forecast for years 4 and 5.

30   PRODUCT Q

(a) (i)   Average accounting profit $= \dfrac{12,500 \text{ units} \times £20 \text{ profit} \times 4 \text{ years}}{5 \text{ years}}$

$$= £200,000$$

Average capital employed $= \dfrac{\text{opening balance} + \text{closing balance}}{2}$

$$= £800,000$$

Average accounting rate of return $= \dfrac{£200,000}{£800,000} \times 100\% = 25\%$

(ii)   **Depreciation** should be excluded from **NPV** calculations because it is not a **cash flow.**

The **fixed overheads** are not relevant to the calculations - the question states that there are no fixed costs which are specific to this project.

Contribution per unit = £(80 – 30) =   £50
Annual contribution, years 2 to 5 =   £50 × 12,500 = £625,000

Year	Cash flow £	Discount factor	Present value £
0	(1,500,000)	1.000	(1,500,000)
1	-		
2	625,000	0.694)	
3	625,000	0.579) 1.755	1,096,875
4	625,000	0.482)	
5	725,000*	0.402	291,450
		Net present value	(111,675)

*£625,000 contribution + £100,000 cash receipt from sale of plant and machinery.

(b) *Advantages of the accounting rate of return*

(i) It is easily understood by non-financial managers.

(ii) It is a measure used by external analysts and therefore needs to be monitored by the company.

Disadvantages of the accounting rate of return

(i) It uses subjective accounting profits, which include depreciation and fixed costs.

(ii) It ignores the time value of money and the relative timings of profits.

(iii) There are many different methods of calculation. Therefore, comparisons may be difficult.

Advantages of the net present value method

(i) It quantifies the effect of the time value of money on project cash flows.

(ii) It provides a measure which is directly comparable from one project to another.

Disadvantage of the net present value method

It can be difficult to establish an appropriate discount rate.

Net present value is a preferable measure of accounting rate of return. This project should not be undertaken because it produces a negative net present value.

31 TRANSPORT FLEET

> *Tutorial note.* There are three important points to remember when attempting investment appraisal questions.
>
> (a) Cash flows are used in the NPV and payback methods of project appraisal. Profits are used in the ARR method of appraisal.
>
> (b) Cash savings should be treated as cash inflows.
>
> (c) Depreciation is not a cash flow.

(a)

Year	1 £	2 £	3 £	4 £	5 £
Savings of outside organisation's costs	250,000	275,000	302,500	332,750	366,025
Drivers' costs	33,000	35,000	36,000	38,000	40,000
Repairs and maintenance	8,000	13,000	15,000	16,000	18,000
Other costs (W)	10,000	15,000	20,000	16,000	22,000
	51,000	63,000	71,000	70,000	80,000
Net savings	199,000	212,000	231,500	262,750	286,025

Working

Depreciation

	£
Cost of fleet	750,000
Final selling price	150,000
Amount to depreciate	600,000

Annual depreciation = £600,000/5 = £120,000

∴ Reduce other costs by £120,000 per annum for inclusion in table.

(b) (i)

Year	Net cash flow £	Cumulative net cash flow £
1	199,000	199,000
2	212,000	411,000
3	231,500	642,500
4	262,750	905,250

The payback therefore occurs in year 4

$$\textbf{Payback period} \quad = 3 + \left(\frac{750,000 - 642,000}{262,750} \right) \text{ years}$$

$$= 3.41 \text{ years}$$

(ii) $\text{ARR} = \dfrac{\text{Estimated average profits / return}}{\text{Estimated average investment}} \times 100\%$

$$\text{Average return} \quad = \frac{\text{Average net savings} - \text{depreciation}}{\text{Life of project}}$$

$$= £\left(\frac{1,191,275 - 600,000}{5} \right) = £118,255$$

$$\text{Average investment} \quad = £\left(\frac{750,000 + 150,000}{2} \right) = £450,000$$

$$\textbf{ARR} = \frac{118,255}{450,000} \times 100\% = 26.3\%$$

(iii)

Year	Cash flow £	Discount factor 12%	Present value £
0	(750,000)	1.000	(750,000)
1	199,000	0.893	177,707
2	212,000	0.797	168,964
3	231,500	0.712	164,828
4	262,750	0.636	167,109
5	286,025	0.567	162,176
5	150,000	0.567	85,050
		Net present value	175,834

(c)   REPORT

To: Investment Manager
From: Cost Accountant
Date: 18 January 20X5
Subject: Transport fleet investment

Following our meeting earlier in the week I have considered the figures associated with
the transport fleet investment and the alternative project and, using these figures, have

calculated results for the two projects as follows.

	Transport fleet	*Alternative*
Payback period	3.41 years	3 years
Accounting rate of return	26.3%	30%
Net present value	£175,834	£140,000

The alternative project has a smaller payback period and a higher accounting rate of return than the transport fleet investment project. It is, however, the net present value method of appraisal which is the most important project appraisal method and the transport fleet investment project has a higher net present value than the alternative project.

The net present value method of project appraisal considers all relevant cash flows associated with a project over the whole of its life and adjusts those occurring in future years to 'present value' by discounting them. The net present value method therefore ensures that the investor will be compensated for the length of time he must wait until the returns are made. The ARR method of appraisal, on the other hand, does not take account of the timing of cash flows and the payback period method of appraisal does not consider all cash flows relating to a project.

Investment in the transport fleet should therefore be undertaken in preference to the alternative project because of its higher net present value.

The only occasion when the alternative project would be preferred is if the firm's objectives were to minimise risk by limiting the exposure of the investment rather than to maximise returns. The alternative project would be preferred because it pays back quicker than the transport fleet investment project.

32 GT COMPANY

> *Tutorial note.* We are given the savings in the form of cash costs therefore there is no need to make any adjustments before using them in the investment appraisal. The cash flows for each year are equal, therefore the payback period can be determined by simply dividing the annual cash flow into the initial investment. The even cash flows also mean that you can take a short cut to calculate the present value of the cash savings, by summing the discount factors and multiplying the total by £2,800.

(a) (i) **Payback period** $= \dfrac{£11,000}{£2,800}$

$=$ 3.9 years, assuming that cash flows occur evenly during the year

(ii)

	£
Present value of cash savings (£2,800 × 5.2162)	14,605
Less initial investment	11,000
Net present value	3,605

(b) (i) Based on the calculations in (a), the firm should invest in the new machine because it results in a **positive net present value** at the desired rate of return of 14%.

The final decision may depend on management's attitude to **risk**, and the ability of the company to wait until the end of the fourth year before recovering the cash invested in the machine.

(ii)   **Non-financial factors** which the firm would need to consider are as follows.

    (1)   The reliability of the machine

    (2)   The arrangements for the maintenance of the machine

    (3)   The quality of the output from the machine

    (4)   The long-term market for the output produced on the machine

    (5)   The effect on staff morale, especially if the machine is difficult to operate or if redundancies would result from its purchase

    (6)   The possible requirement for staff training to enable the efficient operation of the machine

(c)

REPORT

To: GT Company management
From: Cost Accountant
Date: 1 June 20X5
Subject: Proposed incentive scheme

This report details the economic advantages of adopting the proposed incentive scheme.

The table below shows that the total cost per unit of good output will be reduced if the new scheme is adopted.

Fixed production overhead cost per employee day = $8 \times £4 = £32$.

	Units of good output per day		Overhead cost per unit £		Labour cost per unit £	Total cost per unit £
Present scheme	15	(£32/15)	2.13	(£42/15)	2.80	4.93
Proposed scheme	16	(£32/16)	2.00		2.92	4.92
	17		1.88		2.98	4.86
	18		1.78		3.04	4.82
	19		1.68		3.10	4.78
	20		1.60		3.16	4.76

Assuming that the scheme is successful in motivating employees to increase their output levels, the total cost per unit will be reduced despite the increases in the remuneration per unit. This is because the fixed overhead will be spread over a larger volume of output.

It is assumed that employees would still be paid at current levels for achieving an output of 15 units per day, therefore the company should be successful in negotiating the changes with the employees' representatives.

As long as the company is able to sell the increased output at current prices, it would be economically advantageous to adopt the proposed scheme.

33   PROJECTS T AND R

> *Tutorial note.* Part (b)(i) of the question required you to determine whether machinery should be replaced. This simply meant that you had to calculate the net present value of the inflows resulting from the new machinery and the cost of the new machinery but at present day values since the decision is to be made now and not in three years time.

(a)   The **net present value** method of investment appraisal is considered technically superior to payback period and accounting rate of return appraisal methods because it takes account of the time value of money.

The time value of money means that £1 received now is worth more to the individual/ organisation than £1 received in n years time. This is because the £1 received now can be invested today and earn interest so that its quantitative value in n years time is greater than its value now. There is therefore an opportunity cost attached to the delay of cash receipts since there will be an alternative investment opportunity forgone. Net present value appraisal techniques, however, incorporate the concept of the time value of money by discounting all future cash flows back to their present day value using a rate called the cost of capital. The project's net present value is the sum of all the discounted cash inflows and outflows. The quantitative worth at today's values allows a ranking of projects to be carried out: the project with the highest net present value is the most advantageous to the individual/organisation.

There is an obvious advantage to the **payback period** and **accounting rate of return** methods of appraisal: they are relatively straightforward and easy to understand. There are, however, several disadvantages to their use.

The payback method ignores any cash flows that occur after the project has paid for itself. A project that takes time to get off the ground but earns substantial profits once it is established might therefore be rejected if the payback method is used.

The accounting rate of return method is based on accounting profits rather than cash and it may therefore give too much emphasis to notional costs which are merely accounting conventions and not truly relevant to a project's performance. There are also differing views about the way in which ARR should be calculated.

Most importantly, both methods ignore the **time value of money**.

None of these objections apply to the net present value method: it is a technically superior method of investment appraisal.

(b) (i) To assess whether the machinery should be replaced at the end of year 3, we need to ascertain whether the net present value of the cash inflows following replacement is greater than the initial cost.

The profits include depreciation of £75,000/3 = £25,000. Cash flows are therefore £25,000 pa greater than profits.

Year	Cash flow £	Discount factor	Present value £
3	(75,000)	0.675	(50,625)
4	35,000	0.592	20,720
5	28,000	0.519	14,532
6	27,000	0.465	12,555
		NPV =	(2,818)

The machine should therefore not be replaced because the **net present value** of the case inflows resulting from the purchase are less than the net present value of the purchase. The machinery does not generate enough income to cover its purchase price in present value terms.

(ii) (1) The profits of project T include depreciation of $\dfrac{£70,000 - £10,000}{5}$ = £12,000.

∴ Cash flows are £12,000 per annum greater than profits.

	Cash flows	
Year	T	R
	£'000	£'000
1	27	40
2	30	45
3	32	45
4	44	
5	40*	
Cost	70	60
Payback period	2.41 years	1.44 years

*Includes sale proceeds of £10,000

(2)

Year	T Cash flow £'000	R Cash flow £'000	Discount factor	T Present value £	R Present value £
0	(70)	(60)	1.000	(70,000)	(60,000)
1	27	40	0.877	23,679	35,080
2	30	45	0.769	23,070	34,605
3	32	45	0.675	21,600	30,375
4	44		0.592	26,048	
5	40		0.519	20,760	
			Net present value	45,157	40,060

> *Tutorial note.* Because we are not replacing the machine, project R runs for 3 years only.

Project T should be invested in because, although project R has the shorter payback period, project T has the higher net present value.

(c) The discount rate of 14% represents the firm's **cost of capital** which could be the weighted average cost of the sources of capital which the company uses to finance the project or it could be the weighted average of the return required by shareholders and loan stock investors. It could also be the **opportunity cost** of an investment opportunity foregone (that is, the rate of interest that could have been earned on an investment) that was the next best alternative for the company.

34   HOTEL GROUP

> *Tutorial note.* In this question you will have to identify the relevant costs to be included in the calculations. This involves making some assumptions. It is usual to assume that fixed costs remain unaltered and that allocated costs are not relevant, but it is imperative that you state such assumptions.
>
> Remember that depreciation is not a cash flow and should be excluded from present value and payback calculations.

(a) *Assumption.* The allocated costs are **central fixed costs** which are incurred by the hotel group regardless of which machine is used to manufacture the pies.

	£/pie
Selling price	3.00
Variable costs	1.25
Contribution per pie	1.75

BPP PUBLISHING

Year	Annual contribution £ (a)	Discount factor	Present value £
1	70,000	0.833	58,310
2	70,000	0.694	48,580
3	52,500	0.579	30,398
4	35,000	0.482	16,870
5	35,000	0.402	14,070
	Present value of contribution		168,228
	Capital cost		150,000
(a)(ii)	Net present value		18,228

From column (a), **payback period** = 2 years + (10/52.5 × 1 year)
= 2.2 years (i)

(b) If the existing machinery could be sold for £130,000, the net capital cost of the new machine is reduced to £(150,000 – 130,000) = £20,000.

∴ Revised **net present value** = £(168,228 – 20,000)
= £148,228

If the hotel group continues with the old machine:

	£/pie
Selling price	3.00
Variable costs	1.50
Contribution per pie	1.50

Year	Annual contribution £	Discount factor	Present value £
1	60,000	0.833	49,980
2	60,000	0.694	41,640
3	45,000	0.579	26,055
4	30,000	0.482	14,460
5	30,000	0.402	12,060
		Net present value	144,195

The **net present value** for the new machine exceeds that of continuing with the old machine by £(148,228 – 144,195) = £4,033. The existing machine should therefore be replaced by the new machine.

(c) **Other factors** to be considered before accepting the offer:

(i) The **quality** of the outside caterer's pies (Is it consistent?)

(ii) The **reliability** of the caterer (Will supplies be received on time with no delays or problems?)

(iii) The effect on the **morale** of the hotel group's own staff if work is passed to an outside caterer

(iv) Possible future **increases** in the caterer's **price** (Can a fixed price be agreed?)

(v) Other uses for the **space** being used to manufacture pies

(vi) Whether all **allocated costs** will be saved if production is discontinued

(vii) What the effect will be on **stockholdings** of pies

35   PRINTING

> *Tutorial note.* Calculating the NPV means looking at all of the relevant cash outflows and inflows. The penalty payment is relevant to the decision because it will only be incurred if the proposal is adopted. The present value of the annual cash inflows is calculated using the sum of the discount factors for years 1 to 4. To calculate the payback period, we are concerned with the non-discounted cashflows.

(a)   *Initial cash outflow*

	£
Penalty payment	4,000
Machines purchased	12,400
	16,400

Annual net cash inflow

	£
Annual saving	33,000
Operating costs	(27,200)
Net incremental income (£1,600 × 70%)	1,120
	6,920

Net present value

	£
Present value of cash inflows for four years	
£6,920 × 3.04	21,037
Initial outflow	(16,400)
Net present value	4,637

(b)   **Payback period** $= \dfrac{£16,400}{£6,920} = 2.4$ years, assuming even cash flows

The **advantages** of the payback method include the following.

(i)   It is simple to calculate and understand.

(ii)   It helps to preserve an organisation's liquidity, by focusing on early cash flows.

(iii)   It helps to reduce risk, since it places less emphasis on later cash flows, which can be difficult to forecast with any certainty.

The **disadvantages** include the following.

(i)   It ignores cash flows after the payback period. These may be substantial and potentially large profits may be forgone.

(ii)   It does not help to distinguish between proposals which have the same or similar payback periods.

(iii)   It does not quantify the time value of money, ie the fact that cash received earlier can be re-invested by the organisation.

36   FUTURISTIC LTD

Workings

(1)   As the **money rate** given is a round figure, cash flows have been inflated up to actual amounts saved and discounted with this money rate. Alternatively a **real rate of return** could be calculated using the formula $1 + r = \dfrac{1 + m}{1 + i}$ for each type of cash flow and these rates used to discount the cash flows as given in the question. Either way the NPV obtained should be the same.

Year	Equipment (3% pa) £	Labour savings (10% pa) £	Materials savings (5% pa) £	Total £
1	-	22,000	4,200	26,200
2	-	36,300	6,615	42,915
3	-	33,275	5,788	39,063
4	-	36,603	6,078	42,681
5	23,185	40,263	6,381	69,829

(a) *NPV calculation*

Year	Cash flow £ (W1)	Discount factor at 20%	Present value £
0	(105,000)	1.000	(105,000)
1	26,200	0.833	21,825
2	42,915	0.694	29,783
3	39,063	0.579	22,617
4	42,681	0.482	20,572
5	69,829	0.402	28,071
		NPV =	17,868

(b) *IRR calculation*

As the NPV is positive at 20% try a higher discount rate, say 25%.

Year	Cash flow £ (W1)	Discount factor @ 25%	PV £
0	(105,000)	1.000	(105,000)
1	26,200	0.800	20,960
2	42,915	0.640	27,466
3	39,063	0.512	20,000
4	42,681	0.410	17,499
5	69,829	0.328	22,904
		NPV =	3,829

$$\text{Estimated IRR} = 20\% + \frac{17,868}{(17,868+3,829)} \times (25 - 20)\%$$

$$= 26.4\%$$

(c) The NPV is positive at the cost of capital. Therefore, if the estimates of savings and inflation rates are reliable, the project should be undertaken.

37 CONTRACT LTD

(a) *Expected money cash flows*

	01.01.X7 £	31.12.X7 £	31.12.X8 £	31.12.X9 £
Payments:				
Materials (W1)	9,300	9,765		
Unskilled labour (W2)		4,680	5,148	5,663
Sub-contractor (W3)		520		629
Machinery		2,400	2,400	2,400
	9,300	17,365	7,548	8,692
Receipts		12,000	12,000	21,600
Net cash flows	(9,300)	(5,365)	4,452	12,908

$$\text{Net present value} = -9,300 \times \frac{5,365}{(1.11)} + \frac{4,452}{(1.11)^2} + \frac{12,908}{(1.11)^3}$$

$$= -£1,082$$

As the net present value is negative, the contract is not worthwhile.

Workings

(1) $\quad$ 01.01.X7 $= \; 500 \times £18.60 \qquad\qquad\qquad = \qquad\qquad\qquad$ £9,300

$\qquad\quad$ 31.12.X7 $= \; 500 \times £18.60 \times \dfrac{105}{100} \qquad\quad = \qquad\qquad\qquad$ £9,765

(2) $\quad$ 31.12.X7 $= \; 3 \times 52 \times £30 \qquad\qquad\qquad = \qquad\qquad\qquad$ £4,680

$\qquad\quad$ 31.12.X8 $= \; £4,680 \times \dfrac{110}{100} \qquad\qquad = \qquad\qquad\qquad$ £5,148

$\qquad\quad$ 31.12.X9 $= \; £5,148 \times \dfrac{110}{100} \qquad\qquad = \qquad\qquad\qquad$ £5,663

(3) $\quad$ 31.12.X7 $= \; 13 \times £40 \qquad\qquad\qquad\quad = \qquad\qquad\qquad$ £ 520

$\qquad\quad$ 31.12.X9 $= \; £520 \times \dfrac{(110)^2}{(100)} \qquad\qquad = \qquad\qquad\qquad$ £ 629

(4) Overhead costs are not relevant to the calculations as they are unaffected by acceptance of the contract.

(b) The **net present value method** of appraisal is used because it takes account of the timing of receipts and payments and because it provides a measure of the increase in shareholders' wealth if the project is accepted.

Costs are included on an **opportunity cost (incremental cash flow)** basis. Thus historical costs, eg the cost of the existing stock of material X, and fixed costs, eg overhead expenses, are not included as they are not affected by the decision.

Inflation is dealt with by discounting the actual money cash flows expected, by the company's money cost of capital. An alternative and equivalent, approach would have been to reduce expected cash flows to current (01.01.X7) purchasing power and to discount them at the company's 'real' cost of capital, calculated at 0.037 or 3.7% being $\dfrac{1.11}{1.07} - 1$.

Both versions of the net present value model produce the same answer. The former is preferred because it avoids the great difficulty involved in determining an appropriate purchasing power index for a group of shareholders.

PRACTICE DEVOLVED ASSESSMENT 1

RANE LTD

ANSWERS

SECTION 1

> *Tutorial note.* There are different ways you could set out the schedule required for Task 1(b). The data given shows fixed cost per unit; our suggested schedule calculates total contribution at each selling price and then deducts total fixed costs to arrive at the total annual profit. The AAT Assessor commented that many students failed to recognise that fixed costs are not a function of sales volume.
>
> For Task 2(b), factors other than those given in our suggested solution may be acceptable. The Assessor found that answers for this task, requiring a general commercial awareness, were generally disappointing.

Task 1

(a) Mark-up per unit = £10
     Annual profit = £10 × 25,000 units
                       = £250,000

(b)

	Per unit	Per unit	Per unit
	£	£	£
Selling price	70.00	80.00	90.00
Direct materials	14.00	14.00	16.10
Direct labour	13.00	11.70	11.70
Variable production overhead	4.00	4.00	4.00
Sales commission	7.00	8.00	9.00
Total variable cost	38.00	37.70	40.80
Contribution per unit	32.00	42.30	49.20
Sales volume (units)	20,000	16,000	11,000
	£	£	£
Total contribution	640,000	676,800	541,200
Fixed costs			
Production overhead	200,000	190,000	190,000
Selling and distribution	70,000	70,000	70,000
Administration	50,000	50,000	50,000
Total fixed costs	320,000	310,000	310,000
Annual profit	320,000	366,800	231,200

Task 2

MEMORANDUM

To: Chris Jones
From: A Trainee
Date: 22 June 20X5
Subject: Rane Limited - pricing

(a) *Selling price recommendation*

I have calculated the likely effect on Rane Ltd's profit of a change in selling price. I recommend that the selling price be increased to £80. Although at this price the level of sales will be reduced to 16,000 units, annual profit will be maximised at £366,800.

(b)   *Consequences of operating below full capacity*

If Rane Ltd operates below full capacity (as it will at the recommended level of 16,000 units per annum), the following factors should be taken into account.

(i)   *Utilisation of the spare capacity.* Annual profits will rise even if the spare capacity is left idle but it may be possible to increase profits further still by taking the opportunity to use the spare capacity, for example to manufacture another product.

(ii)   *Effect on employee morale.* A large drop in output from 25,000 units to 16,000 units will involves a large cut in direct labour costs. Resulting staff lay-offs could cause ill-feeling among the workforce.

SECTION 2

Tutorial note. In this section, you need to calculate the numbers of components used per unit by dividing component costs per unit of each product by the cost per component (£2). The Assessor found that many candidates failed to consider contribution per unit of limiting factor and that many omitted workings.

Task

(a)   Firstly, the products will be ranked according to the **contribution per component used.**

	A	B	C	D
	£	£	£	£
Selling price	14	12	16	17
Variable costs per unit	11	11	12	12
Contribution per unit	3	1	4	5
Number of components used per unit	2	1	3	4
Contribution per component	£1.50	£1.00	£1.33	£1.25
Ranking	1	4	2	3

Now, components can be allocated according to the above ranking.

Recommended production schedule for next period

Product	Units	Components used
A	4,000	8,000
C	3,600	10,800
D	900	3,600
		22,400

(b)   The **next period's profit** is calculated below.

Product	Units	Contribution per unit	Total
		£	£
A	4,000	3	12,000
C	3,600	4	14,400
D	900	5	4,500
Total			30,900
contribution			
Fixed costs			8,000
Profit			22,900

SECTION 3

Task 1

(a)

Year	Cash flow £	Discount factor 8%	Present value £
0	(55,000)	1.00	(55,000)
1	18,000	0.93	16,740
2	29,000	0.86	24,940
3	31,000	0.79	24,490
Net present value			11,170

(b)

Year	Cash flow £	Cumulative cash flow £
0	(55,000)	(55,000)
1	18,000	(37,000)
2	29,000	(8,000)
3	31,000	23,000

Payback is achieved during year 3. Assuming that cash flows are even, the payback period can be calculated as follows.

$$2 \text{ years} + \frac{8,000}{31,000} = 2^{1}/_{4} \text{ years, approximately}$$

Task 2

MEMORANDUM

To: Marketing Director
From: Assistant Accountant
Date: 22 June 20X5
Subject: New machine purchase

You have requested more information about the appraisal of the proposed purchase of the new machine.

(a) *Recommendation*

On the basis of the information available, I recommend purchase of the machine. Although the payback period is fairly long at approximately 2 years 3 months, the proposal produces an estimated positive net present value of £11,170.

(b) *Net present value and payback period*

The payback period is the length of time which elapses before the net overall cash flows from the project become positive. The purchase of the machine requires an initial outlay of £55,000. It takes $2^{1}/_{4}$ years for the positive cash flows generated by the project to equal (or 'pay back') this initial investment.

The net present value of a project is the sum of the discounted cash flows of the project. This provides a direct measure of the wealth generated by the investment being appraised.

The process of discounting takes account of both the magnitude of cash flows and their timing. For this project, we have used a discount rate of 8%. For example, £1 at the end of year 1 has a present value of £0.93 when discounted using the 8% discount factor. This indicates that £0.93 now could be invested at 8% to grow to £1.00 by the end of year 1. Similarly £18,000 received at the end of year 1 has a present value of £18,000 × 0.93 = £16,740. Discounted cash flow techniques thus take account of the time value of money.

(c)   *Effects of taxation*

Taxation has three main effects on the cash flows arising from capital expenditure.

Firstly, because profits arising from a project will be taxable, the overall net cash inflows will be reduced by the tax on the profits.

Secondly, there is a timing effect. Tax is usually paid during the year following that in which the profit is made. The discount factor applied to the tax payment should reflect this time lag, which can have a significant effect on the present value of the tax payment.

Thirdly, there is the effect of capital allowances. Depreciation is not allowable against tax, but capital allowances are given instead. The rates of the allowances are determined by the Inland Revenue. Capital allowances will reduce taxable profits and thus will reduce the amount of tax which becomes payable.

PRACTICE DEVOLVED ASSESSMENT 2

NORTH AND SOUTH

ANSWERS

SECTION 1

> *Tutorial note*. For Task 1, some failed to realise that percentage fall in turnover before a loss was made is another way of giving the margin of safety. Task 2 extends the example to consider activity at a given level of profit rather than breakeven.

Task 1

Profitability of milk round

	October £	November £
Turnover	34,720	33,600
Cost of goods sold	26,040	25,200
Contribution	8,680	8,400
Fixed costs	4,500	4,500
Operating profit	4,180	3,900
Breakeven turnover	18,000	18,000
Margin of safety	48.2%	46.4%

Workings

	October £	November £
Operating profit	4,180	3,900
Fixed costs	4,500	4,500
Contribution	8,680	8,400
Turnover	34,720	33,600
Percentage contribution	25 %	25 %
Breakeven point (4,500/0.25)	18,000	18,000
Margin of safety	16,720	15,600
Percentage fall in turnover	48.2%	46.4%

BPP PUBLISHING

Green & Co
Accountants and Registered Auditors
37 Black Street
Anytown

20 December 20X5

Mr A Smith
7 White Street
Anytown

Dear Mr Smith

Thank you for your letter of 16 December about your possible purchase of the milk delivery round. I address your queries in turn below.

The figure for contribution in the profitability statement represents the difference between turnover (the sales value of milk sold) and the total of costs which vary with the level of sales. Other costs, such as the hire of premises or the lease of a vehicle for the milk round, are generally not affected by the amount of milk sold and are called fixed costs. The contribution thus represents the amount which the sale of milk 'contributes' to paying for the fixed costs and to providing profit once all fixed costs are paid for. Given that fixed costs do not change over the 'relevant range' of sales, any increase in contribution leads directly to an increase in profit.

Given a selling price of 40 pence per pint, November sales amounted to 84,000 pints. The breakeven volume is then 45,000 pints. At this selling price, you will need to sell 60,000 pints per month to generate profits of £1,500 per month.

If the selling price is reduced to 38 pence, the breakeven volume moves up to 56,250 pints per month. The monthly sales needed to generate profits of £1,500 per month rises to 75,000 pints.

Sales of over 75,000 pints were achieved in November, but you will need to consider whether this is representative of sales in other months. Seasonal effects may be significant. You will also need to consider the likely effect on sales of cutting the price by 2 pence. The overall market demand for milk is likely to be insensitive to price changes, since milk has few substitutes and limited possible uses. However, consumers may be persuaded to switch from supermarkets to your delivery round for their milk supplies if you reduce prices. On the other hand, the supermarket may respond to your price reduction by cutting their own prices.

Yours sincerely

Green & Co

Workings

Current price per bottle	40p
Contribution percentage	25%
Contribution	10p
Cost per bottle	30p
Prospective contribution (38p price)	8p

	£
Fixed costs	4,500
Required profit	1,500
Required contribution	6,000

Breakeven volume (£4,500/10p)	45,000 pints
November sales volume (£33,600/40p)	84,000 pints

Required contribution	£6,000
Contribution per unit	10p
Required sales volume (£6,000/10p)	60,000 pints

Revised breakeven volume (£4,500/8p)	56,250 pints
Required sales volume (£6,000/8p)	75,000 pints

SECTION 2

Tutorial note. You will have found this section difficult if you are unsure about the concepts of opportunity cost, sunk costs and relevant costs. Revise these topics if necessary.

Task 1

To: Elizabeth Brookes
From: Assistant Management Accountant
Date: 15 December 20X5

CONTRACT COSTING

		£	£
Expenditure			
Material A	1,000 kg @ £7		7,000
Material B	600 @ £16	9,600	
	900 @ £24	21,600	
			31,200
Material C	2,000 @ £8		16,000
Labour	2,000 @ £18		36,000
Machinery	2 machines × 3 months × £2,000		12,000
Minimum bid price			102,200

MEMORANDUM

To: Elizabeth Brookes

From: Assistant Management Accountant

Date: 15 December 20X5

Subject: Calculation of the minimum bid price

The attached contract costing is based on an opportunity cost approach. The opportunity cost of an asset is the cost of its next best alternative use. This approach ensures that only costs relevant to the decision are taken into account in establishing the minimum bid price. Under this approach, a machine with no further use to the enterprise has an opportunity cost equal to the proceeds of selling it. For stock items in continuing use, the opportunity cost will be the replacement cost since if the asset is used on a project, it will need to be replaced. No cost is shown for the development department because the opportunity cost of its use is nil. The department is severely underutilised and its costs will be incurred whether or not the department works on this contract. Therefore, these departmental costs are irrelevant to this decision.

The opportunity cost of Material A is £7 per kilogram, its selling price. The material has no further use for the company and, if it is not used on the contract, the next best alternative is to sell it.

Material B can either be sold for £14 per litre or, if used as a substitute for Material X, would save the company £16 per litre. Use of Material B will mean the company having to spend £16 on an extra litre of Material X and this is therefore the opportunity cost of using existing litres of Material B. The company would have to purchase the additional 900 litres at £24 per litre, and so this current purchase price indicates how much resources the company will have to give up.

The current purchase price is also the appropriate figure to use for Material C, since this material is in regular use. The amount paid for Material C currently in stock is not relevant, since whatever is used on the proposed contract will need to be replaced at the current purchase price.

The cost of grade 2 labour excluding apportioned overhead is £8 per hour. Given that this type of labour is in short supply, the relevant cost of its use on the contract must also include the lost contribution which it would earn in alternatively producing the super. The unit contribution is £102 – £30 – £32 = £40. Since the labour cost is £32, each unit of Super must require 4 hours of grade 2 labour, and so the contribution per labour hour is £10. Therefore, the relevant cost of using grade 2 labour on the contract is £18 per hour.

The depreciation charge is a means of allocating historic costs and is irrelevant to the contract decision. Assuming no repairs will be required, the cost of the use of the machinery for the first three months is nil because they have no alternative use in this period. For the subsequent three months, the possible loss of £18,000 in rental income can be avoided by hiring additional machines for a total cost of £12,000.

General overheads are not relevant to the contract decision because they will be incurred whether or not the contract is undertaken.

SECTION 3

REPORT

To: Divisional Accountant
From : Assistant Management Accountant
Date: 15 December 20X5
Subject: Appraisal of A1 project

The Divisional Director appears to have evaluated the project using the return on investment method, calculating the annual profit and comparing this with the initial outlay. This method has the following limitations.

(a) It uses accounting data which depend on the application of accounting conventions (for example, accruals) and accounting policies (for example, the depreciation method and rate).

(b) It includes depreciation, which is a non-cash item reflecting the allocation of historic costs.

(c) It ignores the timing of cash flows arising from the proposal and therefore the time value of money.

These problems can be overcome by evaluating the proposal using discounted cash flow (DCF) techniques.

The DCF analysis set out in Appendix 1 shows the project to have a positive net present value (NPV) of £45,600 and therefore to be worthwhile given the company's cost of capital. £45,600 represents the value of the project in the equivalent of pounds today, ignoring risks of the project.

If we take project risks into account, the evaluation becomes more complex. Risks tend to increase with time, and the further into the future are cash flows, the more uncertain they are. Partly because of this, many organisations use the discounted payback method to supplement the NPV method. This slows the future time at which the NPV becomes positive.

Appendix 2 estimates the discounted payback period to be 4.4 years, indicating that if the project is terminated before that time, it will not have been worthwhile as the NPV will have been negative.

The discounted payback period does not incorporate a measurement of risk, but it does help to indicate the period over which the company should be reasonably confident about the certainty of project cash flows if it is to undertake the project. Since the method ignores positive cash flows beyond the payback period, it is best used in conjunction with the normal NPV analysis in the evaluation process.

Recommendation

Given a cost of capital of 25%, the expected NPV of the project is positive and so meets the company's requirements for investment projects. However, the discounted payback period is long at approximately 4.4 years, and further consideration should be given to any project risks which could affect cash flows over this period.

Appendix 1: Net present value

End of year	Initial outlay £	Cash from sales £	Expenses £	Net cash flow £	Discount factor	Discounted cash flow £	Cumulative DCF £
0	(600,000)			(600,000)	1.000	(600,000)	(600,000)
1		380,000	(140,000)	240,000	0.800	192,000	(408,000)
2		380,000	(140,000)	240,000	0.640	153,600	(254,400)
3		380,000	(140,000)	240,000	0.512	122,880	(131,520)
4		380,000	(140,000)	240,000	0.410	98,400	(33,120)
5		380,000	(140,000)	240,000	0.328	78,720	45,600
Net present value						45,600	

Expenses comprise: Materials £90,000 + Labour £30,000 + Direct overheads £20,000.

Appendix 2: Discounted payback period

Discounted payback period = 4 years + (33,120/78,720) = 4.4 years (assuming even cashflows in year 5)

This is an estimate of the period after which the expected NPV becomes positive.

PRACTICE DEVOLVED ASSESSMENT 3

QUALITY DATA PRODUCTS

ANSWERS

SECTION 1

> *Tutorial note.* This section is a tough one, even with a 50 minute time allowance. Make sure that you leave some time for the written part of the memo, even if you have got stuck in the calculations.

Task 1

Quality Data Products Ltd: company profitability

	8% price decrease		12% price decrease		Revised product	
	Unit	Total	Unit	Total	Unit	Total
	£	£	£	£	£	£
Sales	46.00	128,800,000	44.00	132,000,000	50.00	150,000,000
Variable material	8.72	(24,416,000)	8.72	(26,160,000)	11.99	(35,970,000)
Variable labour	14.20	(39,760,000)	14.20	(42,600,000)	12.20	(36,600,000)
Variable overhead	4.40	(12,320,0000)	4.40	(13,200,000)	4.40	(13,200,000)
Commission	2.30	(6,440,000)	2.20	(6,600,000)	2.50	(7,500,000)
Contribution	16.38	45,864,000	14.48	43,440,000	18.91	56,730,000
Fixed costs		(40,500,000)		(40,500,000)		(52,500,000)
Operating profit		5,364,000		2,940,000		4,230,000
Sales volume (units)		2,800,000		3,000,000		3,000,000

The **volume of sales** with a 12% price decrease is restricted to the capacity of the manufacturing plant (3,000,000 units - see workings).

Variable material costs reduce to £8.72 with the price decrease due to the 20% discount available.

Workings

The forecast statement can be analysed as follows.

		£ per unit
Turnover	£120,000,000/2,400,000	50.00
Variable material	£26,160,000/2,400,000	(10.90)
Variable labour	£34,080,000/2,400,000	(14.20)
Variable production overhead	£10,560,000/2,400,000	(4.40)
Sales commission (5% of sales)	£6,000,000/2,400,000	(2.50)
		(18.00)

Fixed costs	£
Fixed production overhead absorbed	19,200,000
Add underabsorbed overhead	4,800,000
Total fixed production overhead	24,000,000
Fixed selling expenses	11,500,000
Fixed administration expenses	5,000,000
Total fixed costs	40,500,000

The **maximum capacity** can be calculated as follows.

Production overhead absorbed	£19,200,000
Sales and production units	2,400,000
Production overhead per unit	£8.00
Total production overhead	£24,000,000
Maximum capacity units (£24,000,000/£8)	3,000,000

BPP
PUBLISHING

Practice devolved assessment 3

Task 2

MEMORANDUM

To: Hilary Farmer
From: Management Accountant
Date: 15 June 20X6
Subject: Marketing proposals

The operating profit of Quality Data Products Ltd for the current year is estimated at £2.7 million. The volumes of sales necessary under each of the three proposals to achieve this level of profit are as follows.

	8% price decrease £	12% price decrease £	Revised product £
Fixed costs	40,500,000	40,500,000	52,500,000
Required profit	2,700,000	2,700,000	2,700,000
Total contribution	43,200,000	43,200,000	55,200,000
Unit contribution	£16.38	£14.48	£18.91
Required volume (units)	2,637,363	2,983,426	2,919,091

Before making the final decision, the company should also take into account **non-financial aspects** of the three options. These include the following.

(a) The forecasts of demand with reduced prices may not be realised. For example, if consumers associate quality with price, large reductions may alter their perception of the product and sales may not increase to the level required to make a price reduction worthwhile.

(b) Given that a competitor has entered the market, product improvement may be essential if QDP wishes to remain in the market over the medium-term period.

(c) Above, the cost of the marketing campaign has been reflected in the projected results for a single year. However, the benefits of the campaign may extend into future periods, enhancing future profitability.

(d) Operation at full capacity may not always be possible, as a result of machine breakdowns, labour disputes or stock shortages.

SECTION 2

> *Tutorial note.* Note that the amounts Exta charges to Yetum and Zorba (£69.6m = £17.4m + £52.2m) do not affect the overall profitability of the enterprise, and so do not enter into the calculations. You should also assume that overheads remain unchanged.

Task 1

(a) *Effect on profit of discontinuing Yetum*

	£
Loss of revenue	(20,000,000)
Labour cost saving	3,000,000
Plant overhead cost saving	6,000,000
Y1 destruction costs (50,000 × £70)	(3,500,000)
Decrease in annual profit	(14,500,000)

There is no saving in materials cost since this is a **joint output** of Exta Division.

162

(b)   *Unit profitability of additional Yetum output*

Each additional litre of Yetum requires four litres of X1 to be processed by Exta.

		£
Marginal cost for Exta = $\dfrac{£46,000,000 \times 4}{200,000}$		920
Yetum labour cost per litre = $\dfrac{£3,000,000}{50,000}$		60
Destruction cost for surplus Z1 (£40 × 3 litres)		120
Total extra costs per litre		1,100
Selling price of Yetum (£20,000,000 ÷ 50,000)		400
Loss in contribution per additional litre		700

Assuming unchanged overheads, each additional litre of Yetum produced will reduce profit by £700.

Task 2

REPORT

To:	Finance Director
From:	Management Accountant
Date:	15 June 20X6
Subject:	Evaluation of National Chemicals plc

It is assumed in what follows that the Yetum division would not be closed down.

If production of Zorba is increased in line with the National Chemicals proposal, 40,000 litres of Exta will be required. I have assumed here that the 10,000 additional litres of Yetum produced can be sold as there is an increasing demand. The overall effect is to increase profit by £2,000,000, as shown below.

Financial appraisal

Current price of a litre of Zorba $\dfrac{£90,000,000}{150,000 \text{ units}}$		£600
Price offered for additional 30,000 litres		£300
		£
Marginal cost of extra Exta production (£230 × 40,000)		9,200,000
Marginal labour cost of extra Yetum production (£60 × 10,000)		600,000
Marginal labour cost of Zorba production (£40 × 30,000)		1,200,000
Revenue from Yetum sales (£400 × 10,000)		(4,000,000)
Net cost of extra 30,000 litres of Zorba		7,000,000
Revenue (£300 × 30,000)		9,000,000
Additional profit		2,000,000

Other factors

Before going ahead with the new contract, the **following factors** should also be considered.

(a)   We need to consider if the **capacity of plant** in each of the three divisions will be large enough for the increased production.

(b)   We should check, for example by market research, if all of the additional units of Yetum can be sold. If any cannot, and excess production of Y1 therefore needs to be destroyed, there will be additional **destruction costs** as well as **lost contribution**.

(c)   Allowing a price reduction on the additional 30,000 litres might encourage National Chemicals to negotiate a lower price for all units they purchase. If they cannot obtain Zorba easily from elsewhere and/or if there are no suitable substitutes for Zorba, we may be able to negotiate a **higher price** than £30 for the additional units of Zorba they wish to buy.

SECTION 3

> *Tutorial note*. Your explanations of the NPV technique and of the treatment of taxation should be pitched at an appropriate level for such a client and should not assume too much knowledge.

Task

Brown & Co
Accountants and Registered Auditors
Great Haywood Street
Anytown

H Evans Esq
Director
Metal Parts Ltd
Anytown

15 June 20X6

Dear Mr Evans

Proposed machine purchase

As agreed, I am writing to report on my evaluation of the proposed purchase of an additional machine for your company.

According to my calculations (set out below), the purchase is worthwhile at your cost of capital of 10%, although not to the extent you suggest.

The preferred approach to appraisal of investments is the net present value (NPV) approach, which concentrates on expected actual cashflows, which do not suffer from the distortions of accounting policies which affect the calculation of accounting profits.

The NPV approach also recognises that the value of cashflows lessens the further into the future they are received. This is because £1 now can be invested to gain (compound) interest up to some future date. The 'time value of money' is reflected in investment appraisal by multiplying future cash flows by a discount factor to reduce them to present day equivalent amounts. The discount factor I have used is your cost of capital (10%).

NPV investments appraisals need to incorporate taxation as a cashflow. Taxation is based on taxable profits, not accounting profits. Thus, depreciation is not an allowable expense; instead, capital allowances are substituted in their place. Given that you have no other assets generating capital allowances, there will be a balancing allowance at the end of the life of the machine equal to the difference between the capital cost of the machine and the capital allowance previously claimed.

Taxation is normally payable nine months after the end of the accounting year. To simplify the calculations, I have instead assumed a one year delay in the tax payment.

Tax computation

Year	Profit before depreciation £	Capital allowance £	Taxable profit £	Tax payable @30% £	Payable in year
0	-	30,000	(30,000)	(9,000)	1
1	30,000	22,500	7,500	2,250	2
2	42,000	16,875	25,125	7,538	3
3	54,000	12,656	41,344	12,403	4
4	66,000	37,969	28,031	8,409	5

Investment appraisal

End of year	Operating cashflow £	Tax paid £	Net cashflow £	Discount factor	DCF £
1	30,000	(9,000)	39,000	0.909	35,451
2	42,000	2,250	39,750	0.826	32,834
3	54,000	7,538	46,462	0.751	34,892
4	66,000	12,403	53,597	0.683	36,607
5		8,409	(8,409)	0.621	(5,222)
					134,562
			Cost of machine (year 0)		120,000
			Net present value (NPV)		14,562

The positive NPV indicates that the acquisition is worthwhile assessed in equivalent present-day terms.

Yours sincerely

A Technician

PRACTICE DEVOLVED ASSESSMENT 4

YORK PLC

ANSWERS

SECTION 1

> *Tutorial note.* The Assessor commented that many candidates had only a limited grasp of cost behaviour when expressed in terms of average cost and were thus unable to calculate the level of fixed costs. Parts (b) and (c) of Task 1 were well answered although some candidates were unable to calculate the margin of safety.

Task 1

Working

Packs produced	Cost per Unit £	Total cost £'000	Extra cost for 10,000 packs £'000	Variable cost per unit £
40,000	430	17,200	-	-
50,000	388	19,400	2,200	220
60,000	360	21,600	2,200	220
70,000	340	23,800	2,200	220

(a)　For 40,000 packs:

Fixed costs = Total cost – variable costs

= £17,200,000 – (£220 × 40,000)

= £17,200,000 – £8,800,000

= £8,400,000

(b)　Contribution per pack　= £420 – £220 = £200

Profit　　　　　　= Total contribution – fixed costs

= £200 × 65,000 – £8,400,000

= £13,000,000 – £8,400,000

= £4,600,000

(c)　**Break even volume** = Fixed costs/contribution per pack

= £8,400,000/£200 = 42,000 packs

(d)　**Margin of safety** = (65,000 – 42,000)/65,000 = 35%

Task 2

MEMO

To:　　　Ben Cooper, Marketing Director
From:　　A Technician
Date:　　5 December 20X6
Subject:　Profitability of export order

The effect on profits of accepting the possible export order at the volumes and prices discussed is calculated below. If the order is for 15,000 packs, there is contribution lost from sales at the usual £420 because maximum capacity is reached.

Order for 5,000 packs at £330

Total contribution = Volume × contribution per pack
= 5,000 × (£330 – £220)
= 5,000 × £110
= £550,000

Order for 15,000 packs at £340

Total contribution = Volume × contribution per pack – lost contribution
= 15,000 × (£340 – £220) – 10,000 × £200
= 15,000 × £120 – £2,000,000
= £1,800,000 – £2,000,000
= –£200,000

The calculations show that the order for 5,000 packs contributes £550,000 to profit, while the order for 15,000 packs reduces profits by £200,000. Accordingly, the order for 5,000 packs is to be preferred.

In spite of the higher price for the 15,000 pack order, profits fall because it diverts sales of 10,000 packs which would otherwise be made at the normal higher price of £420. This is because the maximum capacity is 70,000 packs and, given normal sales of 65,000 packs, only 5,000 packs can be supplied from additional production. Accepting the order for 15,000 packs means giving up sales of 10,000 packs with a contribution of £200 per pack.

There are, however, additional non-financial factors which should be considered before a final decision is made.

(a) Existing customers might discover that we had supplied packs at a lower than normal price, and might seek to negotiate lower prices themselves as a result.

(b) If it is possible for the purchaser placing the proposed order to sell packs on into the market, the resulting increased supply of the packs in the market might reduce demand for packs we offer for sale at our normal price.

SECTION 2

Tutorial note. The Assessor commented that a significant minority of candidates wanted to bring in taxation - presumably because this was assessed in the June 1996 Central Assessment - while a similar number insisted on seven years of cashflows simply because there were seven years of growth and seven years of discount factors provided.

REPORT

To: Chief Executive
From: A Technician
Date: 5 December 20X6
Subject: Replacement of laundry equipment

An evaluation of the two options being considered - purchase of machine A and rental of machine B - is set out below, using the discounted cash flow (DCF) method.

Forecast annual laundry volume increase = 10%, for the next seven years.

Machine A

Years from now	Volume kg	Variable costs £	Fixed costs £	Total cost £	Discount factor	Discounted cost £
1	145,200	726,000	20,000	746,000	0.870	649,020
2	159,720	798,600	20,000	818,600	0.756	618,862
3	175,692	878,460	20,000	898,460	0.658	591,187
						1,859,069
Add capital cost payable now						60,000
Net present cost						1,919,069

Machine B

Years from now	Volume kg	Variable costs £	Fixed Costs £	Total cost £	Discount factor	Discounted cost £
1	145,200	755,040	38,000	793,040	0.870	689,945
2	159,720	830,544	38,000	868,544	0.756	656,619
3	170,000	884,000	38,000	922,000	0.658	606,676
3	5,692	56,920		56,920	0.658	37,453
Net present cost						1,990,693

Using the hospital's required rate of return of 15%, the evaluation shows the purchase of machine A to be preferable to rental of machine B. The net present cost for machine A is approximately £1,919,000, which is £72,000 less than the £1,991,000 cost for machine B.

A further benefit of choosing machine A is that it has surplus capacity taking into account forecast volume increases. This would be helpful in keeping costs down if actual laundry volume turns out to be higher than the levels forecast.

The residual value of £10,000 for the existing equipment has been ignored because it is not relevant to the choice between machine A and machine B. The funds of £10,000 will be received whichever new machine is chosen.

The DCF method used takes into account the time value of money. Even in the absence of inflation and risk, money has a time value because consumption now is generally preferred to future consumption. As a result, investors require a reward to compensate them for deferring consumption and borrower have to pay compensation in exchange for receiving cash now instead of in the future.

It follows from this that a pound in the future has less value than a pound now. The further into the future that a flow of cash occurs, the lower will be its value in present day terms. DCF reflects this by using factors to discount cash flows to present values. Cash flows in different time periods can, when discounted, be added together to find the total net present value or cost of a project.

PRACTICE DEVOLVED ASSESSMENT 5

BRITA BEDS LTD

ANSWERS

SECTION 1

> *Tutorial note*. In tasks like this on breakeven analysis and limiting factors, it is important to recognise the significance of the concept of contribution, a word which is not mentioned in the assessment.

Task 1

(a) Contribution required to break even = fixed costs

= £8,450 + £10,000 + £40,000 + £40,000

= £98,450

Mix of models

A:B:C

3:4:3

3As + 4Bs + 3Cs = 10 beds

Contribution per batch of 10 beds

	£
Sales	
As (£208 × 3)	624
Bs (£351 × 4)	1,404
Cs (£624 × 3)	1,872
	3,900
Cost of beds (£3,900 ÷ 1.3)	(3,000)
Commission	(390)
Transport	(400)
Contribution	110

Breakeven point = £98,450 ÷ £110 = 895, ie 8,950 beds

(b) 895 batches of 10 beds represent **turnover** of:

£3,900 × 895 = £3,490,500

Task 2

Workings

(a)

	£
Loss of interest (£300,000 × 0.05)	15,000
Loss of salary	36,550
	51,550

(b) Fixed costs = £98,450 – £40,000 = £58,450

Contribution required = 58,450 + 51,550 = £110,000

£110,000 ÷ £110 = 1,000 batches, ie 10,000 beds

(c) *Likely maximum annual sales*

	£
2.1 × 44,880 × 10% × 1/9 =	1,047
2.1 × 44,880 × 60% × 1/10 =	5,655
2.1 × 44,880 × 30% × 1/11 =	2,570
	9,272

Smith, Williams & Jones
42 The Esplanade
Belltown
BL4 2NP

24 June 20X7

Ms J Howarth
24 Endsleigh Road
Belltown BL6 4PP

Dear Ms Howarth

BRITA BEDS LIMITED

Than you for your letter of 18 June about the possible purchase of Brita Beds Limited. Before calling you to arrange a meeting, I thought it might be useful to set out some relevant figures.

By purchasing the business for £300,000, you will sacrifice interest at 5% on £15,000, as well as your current salary of £36,550, making the profit required £51,550 in total. £40,000 will be saved in manager's salary costs.

To cover the new reduced fixed costs and to achieve the required level of profit, the company will need to sell 10,000 beds in the current mix of models.

Based on the market research information available, the likely annual sales of beds in Mytown will be 9,272 units. This would represent a shortfall of 728 units below the profit level required, equivalent to approximately £8,000 in profit.

The information available suggests that you should not purchase the company because it is likely that your income will drop by £8,000 if you do so.

Having said that, it should be noted that the market research estimates could prove inaccurate, for example because of the following.

(a)   The population of the area may change in the future, and this will change the likely demand for beds.

(b)   A competitor might set up a rival outlet in the town at some stage in the future, and take some of Brita's market share.

The uncertainties in the market research forecast underline the riskiness of the venture and tend to support my advice not to proceed with the venture.

I look forward to meeting you soon to discuss these matters further.

Yours sincerely

A Technician

Task 3

(a)   It is assumed that one month's sales needs to be stored.

First, we confirm that storage space is a **limiting factor**.

Storage required = $35 \times 3 + 45 \times 4 + 20 \times 5 = 385\text{m}^2$. 300m^2 only is available.

Next, we calculate **contribution earned per unit of storage space**.

	A £	B £	C £
Selling price	240.00	448.00	672.00
Unit cost	(130.00)	(310.00)	(550.00)
Carriage	(20.00)	(20.00)	(20.00)
Unit contribution	90.00	118.00	102.00
Storage per bed (m²)	3	4	5
Contribution per m²	£30	£29.50	£20.40
Priority	1st	2nd	3rd

Production schedule

	m²
A (35 × 3)	105
B (45 × 4)	180
C (balance: 3 × 5)	15
	300

Recommended monthly sales schedule

Model	Number of units
A	35
B	45
C	3

(b)

	A £	B £	C £	Total £
Sales	8,400	20,160	2,016	30,576
Unit costs	(4,550)	(13,950)	(1,650)	(20,150)
Carriage	(700)	(900)	(60)	(1,660)
Contribution	3,150	5,310	306	8,766
Staff costs				(3,780)
Department overheads				(2,000)
General overheads				(2,520)
Profit				466

SECTION 2

SOUND EQUIPMENT LTD

To: Financial Director
From: Assistant Accountant
Date: 24 June 20X7
Subject: Proposal to build amplifier for JBZ plc

Introduction

The purpose of this report is to appraise the JBZ plc proposal using the net present value technique. The technique takes account of the time value of money by discounting cash flows at the company's cost of capital.

The net present value of a project is the sum of the discounted cash flows: this provides a direct measure in present value terms of the wealth generated by the proposal.

Taxation

Like the operating cash flows - sales revenue and payments to suppliers for materials and labour - corporation tax payments represent a flow of cash, with a delay of one year. Depreciation must not be deducted in arriving at taxable profits. Instead, capital allowances, the equivalent of depreciation for tax purposes - must be calculated and accounted for. In the Appendix, tax on income less capital allowances is calculated for each year and then entered into the table for overall cash flows.

Conclusion

The calculations in the Appendix show the project to have a negative net present value (NPV) of £2,913 with corporation tax at 30%, suggesting that the contract should not be accepted. However, the negative NPV is relatively small. One factor which you may wish to consider before making a final decision is the possibility of follow-on opportunities if the contract is accepted. It has been mentioned that subsequent contracts may be available: if the proposal is not accepted now, the company may forego the possibility of being considered for these contracts, which could have significantly positive benefits.

Appendix

Capital allowances

Year	Allowance £	Reducing balance £
1	37,500	112,500 (150,000 – 37,500)
2	28,125	84,375 (112,500 – 28,125)
3	84,375	

Operating cash flows

Year	1 £	2 £	3 £
Sales	180,000	180,000	180,000
Materials	(60,000)	(63,000)	(66,150)
Labour	(40,000)	(42,000)	(44,100)
	80,000	75,000	69,750
Capital allowances	(37,500)	(28,125)	(84,375)
Taxable	42,500	46,875	(14,625)
Tax at 30%	(12,750)	(14,063)	4,388
In year:	2	3	4

Overall cash flows

Year	Equipment £	Operating cash flows £	Tax £	Net cash flow £	Discount factor 18%	PV £
0	(150,000)			(150,000)	1.000	(150,000)
1		80,000		80,000	0.847	67,760
2		75,000	(12,750)	62,250	0.718	44,696
3		69,750	(14,063)	55,687	0.609	33,913
4			4,388	4,388	0.516	2,264
Net present value						(1,367)

PRACTICE DEVOLVED ASSESSMENT 6

FORTUNE PLC

ANSWERS

SECTION 1

Task 1

(a) *Budgeted sales volume in litres*

	£'000
Production fixed overheads absorbed	640
Production fixed overheads unabsorbed	160
Total production fixed overheads	800

Maximum capacity = maximum sales (litres)   100,000
Budgeted capacity = budgeted sales (litres) [(640/800) × 100,000]   80,000

(b) *Break-even point*

Fixed costs	£'000
Production fixed overheads	800
Fixed selling expenses	600
Fixed administration expenses	400
Total fixed costs	1,800

Contribution	£'000
Turnover	16,000
Variable material	6,400
Variable labour	3,200
Variable overhead	1,600
Commission	800
Total contribution	4,000

Unit contribution	£50
Break-even point (litres) (£1.8m / £50)	36,000

Contribution percentage (£4m / £16m)	25%
Break-even point (£)	£7.2m

(c) *Percentage decrease in budgeted sales to achieve break-even*

Units	
Current sales (litres)	80,000
Break-even sales (litres)	36,000
	44,000

Percentage decrease [(44/80) × 100]	55%

Alternative answer:	£'000
Value	16,000
Current sales	7,200
Break-even sales	8,800

Percentage decrease [(£8.8m/£16m) × 100]	55%

Workings   Selling price = marginal cost per litre + contribution per litre = £60 + £40 = £100

MEMO

To: Sales Manager   **From:**   Assistant Management Accountant
          Colouring Division   Head Office

Date: 4 December 20X7

Subject: Budget preparation

I note that you have not yet been able to prepare a budget for the year to 31 December 20X8. To help you, I have identified the budgeted sales and profit from existing customers and have analysed the financial implications of the possible special order. Before deciding whether or not to accept the special order, the non-financial implications should also be considered.

(a)   **Budgeted turnover and profit excluding the special offer**

	£'000
Turnover [£100 × 100,000 litres]	10,000
Marginal cost [60 × 100,000]	6,000
Contribution	4,000
Fixed costs	2,400
Budget profit before special order	1,600

(b)   **Evaluation of special order**

   (i)   *Without external sourcing*

Order volume (litres)	30,000
Unit contribution [£90 − £60]	£30
Gross contribution [£30 × 30,000]	£900,000
less contribution lost from existing customers [£40 × 10,000]	£400,000
Net contribution on accepting special order when sourced internally	£500,000

   (ii)   *With external sourcing*

Contribution from internally sourced production [£30 × 20,000]	£600,000
Contribution per litre from external sources [£90 − £105 = − £15]	
Contribution from externally sourced production [− £15 × 10,000]	(£150,000)
Net contribution on accepting special order when sourced internally	£450,000

(c)   **Non-financial issues to be considered**

Although the best option seems to be to accept the special order and source all production internally, before making a final decision the following issues should be considered:

   (i)   Loss of goodwill from failure fully to satisfy demand from existing customers if production of the special order is sourced entirely from within the division

   (ii)   The possibility of existing customers becoming aware of reduced prices and demanding similar terms whichever option is chosen

   (iii)   The effect of the reduced price on the image of the Colouring Division

   (iv)   A possible lowering of overall divisional profitability if the new customer takes an increasing proportion of output at the expense of existing, more profitable customers

   (v)   The supplier becoming aware of the Colouring Division's markets

Task 3

The notes should include the following.

(a) *Minimum contract price*

Proposed contract – revised cost

	Notes	£
Material A	1	28,000
Material B	2	55,000
Labour	3	1,000
General divisional overheads	4	nil
Minimum price for the contract		84,000

Notes

		£	£
1	£28 × 1,000 kg		28,000
2	500 kg	13,000	
	1,500 kg @ £28	42,000	
			55,000
3	900 hours	nil	
	100 hours @ £10	£1,000	
			1,000
4	Overheads are not an incremental cost.		

(b) *Technique used to derive the costs of the contract*

The technique used to derive the minimum contract price is known as **opportunity costing**. This measures the cost of a resource as being its value in the next best alternative to its proposed use.

The 'real' cost of a resource is not necessarily how much it costs but, rather, its value to the business. This can often be measured by calculating how worse off the business would be if it was deprived of the resource.

(c) *Justification for the cost of labour and divisional fixed overheads*

Using the information provided, the **opportunity cost** of the fixed overheads and the 900 hours of labour is nil if these are surplus and have no other possible uses. The amount of these expenses is the same whether or not the contract is undertaken. There is therefore **no extra cost** to the division if they are used in the contract. The only extra cost will be the 100 hours of overtime because accepting the contract directly involves cash leaving the business.

REPORT

To: Ann Spring   **From:** Accounting Technician
Date: 4 December 20X7

Subject: *Investment proposal and the internal rate of return*

(a) and (b) Calculation of net present value at 30% and 70% discount rates

INVESTMENT APPRAISAL – CALCULATION OF NET PRESENT VALUES

End of year	Units	Cash received £	Material £	Labour £	Rent £	NCF £	Factor 30%	DCF £	Factor 70%	DCF £
1	10,000	420,000	200,000	150,000	20,000	50,000	0.769	38,450	0.588	29,400
2	11,000	462,000	220,000	150,000	20,000	72,000	0.592	42,624	0.346	24,912
3	12,100	508,200	242,000	152,000	20,000	94,200	0.455	42,861	0.204	19,217
4	13,310	559,020	266,200	176,200	20,000	96,620	0.350	33,817	0.120	11,594
								157,752		85,123
Initial cost								100,000		100,000
Net present value								57,752		(14,877)

(c)   Calculation of the internal rate of return

$$\text{Internal rate of return} = 30\% + \left(\frac{57,752}{57,752 + 14,877} \times (70\% - 30\%) \right)$$

$$= 61.8\%$$

(d)   The meaning of the internal rate of return

The internal rate of return is the discount rate which reduces the net present value of a proposed cashflow stream to zero. For a traditional investment comprising an outflow followed by inflows, if the internal rate of return is greater than the required return then the proposal is worthwhile.

TRIAL RUN DEVOLVED ASSESSMENT 1

ALLBRIGHT METALS

ANSWERS

Task 1

The following costs will be disallowed.

1   75% of the cost of the Project Director
2   50% of the cost of the Lab Technician
3   IT department overhead apportionment
4   Library apportionment
5   Departmental overhead
6   £750 of the training costs
7   Secretary's salary
8   Administrator's salary
9   Laboratory refurbishment

Further adjustments are required to the figures as follows.

1   The salary costs will all be increased by 10% to allow for national insurance contributions.

2   Overhead will be calculated at a rate of 40% of the total revised research staff costs (£8,250 + £17,600 + £15,400).

REVISED RESEARCH BUDGET

	£
Salaries:	
Project Director	8,250
Researcher 1	17,600
Researcher 2	15,400
Lab technician	6,050
Sub-total	47,300
Expenses:	
Laboratory consumables	5,000
Travel	800
Conferences	2,300
Training	1,050
Overhead	16,500
Sub-total	25,650
Capital costs:	
Purchase of filtration equipment	3,500
Adaptation of compactor	2,200
Purchase of magnetic separator	15,000
Sub-total	20,700
Total	93,650

MEMO

Date: dd.mm.yy

To: Professor Z Goran
          Derwent University

From: Nathan King
          Engineering Research Council

Subject: Iron and Lead Extraction Project – Research Budget

Thank you for the research proposals that you submitted recently. I have been looking in some detail at your research budget for the project. Although very comprehensive, it appears to be out of line with the ERC expenditure guidelines in a number of areas as follows.

1   Only the marginal cost of research staff is allowed. This means that only the time that they spend working on the project may be allocated to the project, even if they have been recruited as a consequence of the project being undertaken. Thus, in this case 50% of the cost of the Lab Technician and 75% of the cost of the Project Director should be excluded.

2   The full cost of their employment may be included. This means that the NI costs can be added to the salary costs.

3   No overhead costs may be apportioned directly to the project. This means that the cost of support services, including secretarial help, library and IT services must be excluded.

4   The ERC operates a policy of overhead recovery at a rate of 40% of research staff costs. This allowance is intended to cover the overhead that would be attributable to the average project of this type.

5   The cost of supervising the second researcher for his master's degree must also be excluded since this item is not required in order for the project to go ahead.

6   The laboratory refurbishment cost must be excluded, since this would be required whatever the laboratory was used for.

The effect of these changes is to reduce the total research budget to £93,650. This reduction can be summarised as follows.

	£
Change in treatment of overheads (£24,300-£16,500)	7,800
Reduction in training cost	750
Laboratory refurbishment	6,000
Change in research and lab staff costs	23,700
Total reduction	38,250

If you would like to discuss these figures further, please do not hesitate to contact me.

Task 2

Calculation of annual labour costs

Year	Pay index	£10,000 ×	Actual cost
0	135	135/135	10,000
1	139	139/135	10,296
2	144	144/135	10,667
3	149	149/135	11,037
4	155	155/135	11,481

Calculation of capital allowances	£
Capital cost	30,000
Writing down allowance – year 1	(7,500)
Balance	22,500
Writing down allowance – year 2	(5,625)
Balance	16,875
Writing down allowance – year 3	(4,219)
Balance	12,656
Balancing allowance	(12,656)

Calculation of contribution and tax	Year 1	Year 2	Year 3	Year 4
Savings on waste disposal costs	11,000	11,000	11,000	11,000
Labour	(10,296)	(10,667)	(11,037)	(11,481)
Power	(1,200)	(1,500)	(1,500)	(1,500)
Membranes	(3,000)	(6,000)	(6,000)	(6,000)
Contribution	(3,496)	(7,167)	(7,537)	(7,981)
Capital allowances	(7,500)	(5,625)	(4,219)	(12,656)
Taxable profit/(loss)	(10,996)	(12,792)	(11,756)	(20,637)
Corporation tax at 30%	3,299	3,838	3,527	6,191
Due in year:	2	3	4	5

NPV investment appraisal

	Year 0	Year 1	Year 2	Year 3	Year 4	Year 5	Total
Capital payments	(30,000)						(30,000)
Contribution		(3,496)	(7,167)	(7,537)	(7,981)		(26,181)
Corporation tax			3,299	3,838	3,527	6,191	16,854
Net cash flow	(30,000)	(3,496)	(3,868)	(3,699)	(4,454)	6,191	(39,327)
20% discount factors	1.000	0.833	0.694	0.579	0.482	0.402	
Discounted cash flow	(30,000)	(2,912)	(2,684)	(2,142)	(2,147)	2,489	(37,397)

The **NPV** cost of the proposal is therefore £37,397.

BPP PUBLISHING

Calculation of breakeven point

Let the required increase in the annual level of waste disposal savings = a
The contribution statement can now be redrafted as follows:

	Year 1	Year 2	Year 3	Year 4	Total
Savings on waste disposal costs	11,000+a	11,000+a	11,000+a	11,000+a	44,000+4a
Labour	−10,296	−10,667	−11,037	−11,481	−43,481
Power	−1,200	−1,500	−1,500	−1,500	−5,700
Membranes	−3,000	−6,000	−6,000	−6,000	−21,000
Contribution	a − 3,496	a − 7,167	a − 7,537	a − 7,981	4a − 26,181

For the pilot plant to breakeven in operational terms, the contribution must equal zero:

$$4a - 26,181 \qquad 0$$
$$4a \qquad 26,181$$
$$a \qquad 6,545$$

Annual savings in waste disposal costs must therefore increase by £6,545 to **£18,545** for the pilot plant to **break even** in operational terms.

Notes

1   The cost of the feasibility study has been excluded because this is a **sunk cost**.

2   Rent and rates have been excluded because the part of the factory in which the plant will be built is currently unoccupied. There is therefore no **opportunity cost**.

Task 3

MEMO

Date: dd.mm.yy
To: Project Management Committee
From: Nathan King
Subject: Iron and Lead Extraction Project – commercial viability

Attached are schedules of calculations showing the budgeted annual cost statement for the commercial development of this project expressed on an annual basis and on a cost per tonne basis. The cost statement has been combined with the calculations of the savings in waste disposal costs and the income from the recovery of the metals to arrive at a calculation of the expected economic benefits arising from the project being undertaken.

The project is sensitive to changes in the level of landfill tax and to uncertainties as to the value of the lead that will be recovered from the process. The most likely scenario is that the landfill tax situation will be unchanged, and that the price of the lead recovered will be £6 per tonne. On this basis, the project should yield an annual benefit of £11,400, or £5.70 per tonne of inputs and thus should be economically viable, in addition to the environmental benefits that will result.

I have also calculated the effect on the figures of the different scenarios with regard to the landfill tax situation and the lead price. It can be seen that there is a 30% probability that the project could make a small annual loss of £1,600. However, the expected value is £7,600, and therefore on this basis I believe that the project should be allowed to go ahead on economic grounds.

Savings in waste disposal cost per tonne

The current cost per tonne of material disposed is £50. The new process would produce 1,000 tonnes of waste going to landfill at a cost of £12 per tonne. Since there are 2,000 tonnes of sludge going into the process, this is effectively a cost of £6 per tonne of inputs. The saving in disposal costs is therefore £44 per tonne of inputs.

Income per tonne

The new process would produce:

		£
200 tonnes of iron at a price of £5 per tonne:		1,000
400 tonnes of lead at a price of £6 per tonne:		2,400
	Total:	3,400

The income is therefore £1.70 per tonne of inputs to the process (£3,400/2,000).

Budgeted cost statement

	Notes	Total £	Cost/tonne £
Direct costs:			
Labour			
Supervisor		14,000	
Direct labour		28,500	
Sub-total		42,500	21.25
Power	1	14,000	7.00
Membranes	2	5,000	2.50
Sub-total		61,500	30.75
Production overheads:			
Maintenance labour	3	1,350	0.67
Maintenance materials	4	2,250	1.13
Indirect labour	5	3,500	1.75
Other production overheads	6	7,400	3.70
Sub-total		14,500	7.25
Depreciation		4,000	2.00
Total		80,000	40.00

Benefit calculation	Total £	Per tonne £
Savings in waste disposal costs	88,000	44.00
Income from metal recovered	3,400	1.70
Sub-total	91,400	45.70
Process cost	(80,000)	(40.00)
Net benefit	11,400	5.70

Notes

1   The total electricity requirement is 200,000 units ($100 \times 2,000$). This means that the price will be 7p per unit, a total of £14,000.

2   Membranes cost £250 each. If each has a life of 100 tonnes, this means that the annual requirement will be 20 membranes at a total cost of £5,000.

3   Maintenance labour will be allocated on the basis of machine hours. The total machine hours budget is 72,000, of which 1,800 are attributable to the new process. The allocation is therefore £54,000 × 1,800/72,000 = £1,350.

4   Maintenance materials will be allocated on the basis of machine hours. The total machine hours budget is 72,000, of which 1,800 are attributable to the new process. The allocation is therefore £90,000 × 1,800/72,000 = £2,250.

5   Indirect labour costs are allocated on the basis of direct labour hours. Total direct labour hours are 70,000, of which 7,000 are attributable to the new process. The allocation is therefore £35,000 × 7,000/70,000 = £3,500.

6   Other production overhead is allocated on the basis of floor space occupied. Total factory floor space is 20,000 square feet, of which 2,000 square feet will be occupied by the new process. The allocation is therefore £74,000 × 2,000/20,000 = £7,400.

Probability analysis

The effect of the increase in landfill tax would be to increase the costs of disposal by £13 per tonne. This is an increase of £13,000 per 2,000 tonnes of inputs, which would reduce the savings in disposal costs from £88,000 to £75,000.

The effect of the increase in the lead price would be to increase the income from metal recovery by £14 per tonne. This is an increase of £5,600 per 2,000 tonnes of inputs, which would increase the income from metal recovered from £3,400 to £9,000.

The probabilities of these circumstances occurring are shown in the following diagram.

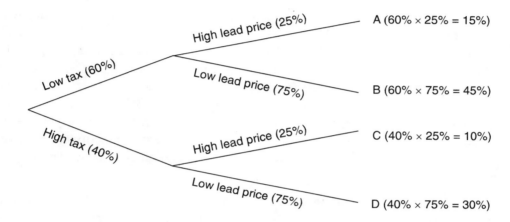

The possible outcomes and their probabilities can be calculated as follows.

	A £	B £	C £	D £	Total
Savings in waste disposal costs	88,000	88,000	75,000	75,000	
Income from metal recovered	9,000	3,400	9,000	3,400	
Sub-total	97,000	91,400	84,000	78,400	
Process cost	(80,000)	(80,000)	(80,000)	(80,000)	
Net benefit	17,000	11,400	4,000	(1,600)	
Probability	0.15	0.45	0.10	0.30	1.00
Probable benefit	£2,550	£5,130	£400	£(480)	£7,600

THE ENGINEERING RESEARCH COUNCIL

FAX TRANSMISSION

To: Ian Stewart
           Managing Director, Allbright Metals plc

From: Nathan King
           Engineering Research Council

Subject: Iron and Lead Extraction Project – pricing to customers

There are a number of areas that will have to be considered in offering this service to customers on a commercial basis. Some of these relate directly to pricing, while others have wider implications. I believe that the main issues that need to be addressed are as follows.

1   **Pricing**

The traditional approach to pricing products and services is **full cost plus pricing**, whereby the sales price is determined by calculating the full cost of the product and adding a percentage mark-up for profit. The problem in this case is that this is a new product that will be competing with a different technology currently offered by the waste disposal companies. Since the cost base of the process will be different, the cost plus approach is likely to produce a price that is in a different range from that offered by the waste disposal companies. In other words, it will either be too cheap, in which case Allbright Metals will not maximise the profit that could be earned, or it will be uncompetitive, in which case there is no incentive for metallurgical companies to change their behaviour with regard to disposal.

Another approach is **marginal cost plus pricing**. This is similar to full cost plus pricing, except that the mark-up is applied to the marginal price of the service rather than the full price. This means that if it is likely that the new process is uncompetitive on a full cost plus basis, a marginal basis could be used to ensure that if the process were offered on the market it would make some contribution to overheads. This approach would not be unreasonable since waste disposal is not a core business and therefore the margin earned by the mainstream products would be unaffected.

2   **Wider commercial and environmental issues**

Allbright Metals must ensure that the plant has sufficient capacity to offer a reliable service to other customers.

Could such an action sour the relationship with Cleanup plc, on whom Allbright Metals will still rely for a significant amount of waste disposal?

Will the Environment Agency be happy with the extension of processing at the plant?

Might there be a problem with local residents if tanker movements increase, and the company is perceived to be processing toxic waste?

TRIAL RUN DEVOLVED ASSESSMENT 2

NORTHOVER SCHOOL

ANSWERS

Task 1

NORTHOVER FIRST SCHOOL - NEXT YEAR'S BUDGET - FIRST DRAFT

Number of children per year			75
Number of children on roll			225
LEA funding per child (capitation)			£920
Special needs budget			£16,000
Number of classes			6
	Notes	£	£
LEA funding:			
Capitation	1		207,000
Special needs			16,000
Sub-total			223,000
Teaching staff:	2		
Headteacher		29,870	
Deputy headteacher		25,750	
Grade 7 teachers	× 2	41,200	
Grade 5 teachers	× 1	18,540	
Grade 3 teachers	× 2	30,900	
Sub-total			146,260
Ancillary staff:	3		
Classroom assistants	× 3	30,939	
Secretary		11,344	
Caretaker		10,313	
Sub-total			52,596
Other costs:			
Stationery	4	12,000	
Books & other resources	5	6,750	
IT support		4,000	
Heating		5,000	
Cleaning		6,000	
Maintenance		4,000	
Sundry		5,000	
Sub-total			42,750
Total costs			241,606
Budget deficit			(18,606)

The first draft of the budget suggests that this school will be in deficit if no changes are made to cost base once the Year 3 pupils have been lost to the middle school. The school will not therefore be financially viable.

Notes

1   The total capitation is now based on three year groups each containing 75 pupils at a rate of £920 per pupil.

2   The budget for teachers' salaries has been increased by 3% as follows:

Headteacher	29,000	+ 3%	29,870
Deputy headteacher	25,000	+ 3%	25,750
Grade 7 teacher	20,000	+ 3%	20,600
Grade 5 teacher	18,000	+ 3%	18,540
Grade 3 teacher	15,000	+ 3%	15,450

3   Ancillary staff salaries have been increased as follows:

Classroom assistant	10,000	× 165/160	10,313
Secretary	11,000	× 165/160	11,344
Caretaker	10,000	× 165/160	10,313

4   Stationery costs have a fixed element of £3,000, and a semi-variable element of £40 per pupil. The cost is therefore £3,000 + (225 × £40) = £12,000.

5   Books and other resources are a fully variable cost at £30 per pupil, giving a total cost of 225 × £30 = £6,750.

Task 2

MEMO

Date: dd.mm.yy

To: Mrs S Parker
         Northover First School

From: Chetna Paul
         Solent Local Education Authority

Subject: Pre-school Class proposals

I have spent some time considering both your school's budget for next year and the pre-school class proposals that you and Sharon Coates have been working on. The figures supplied by Sharon were very helpful, but I should point out that she has used a full absorption costing approach to the problem of overhead allocation. While this approach is valid when we are considering the whole school budget, it is not appropriate for evaluating the impact on the school budget of opening a pre-school class. In this case a marginal costing approach that only takes into account those additional costs that will be incurred in operating the class should be used. This is because overheads such as ancillary staff salaries and heating will be incurred at the budgeted rate, regardless of whether the class is opened or not, and they are therefore not relevant to this decision.

I have redrafted the figures, and these are shown below. You will see that on a marginal costing basis, operating the pre-school class would make a contribution of £6,920 per year towards covering the fixed costs of the school. My first draft of your budget for next year suggests that you could face a deficit of £18,606, and therefore while the pre-school class proposal does not solve this problem in full, it does go some way towards closing the funding gap.

I therefore believe that the pre-school option should be pursued further, and I also think that we should look at other alternative uses for the remaining spare classroom that will be left when the Year 3 children have moved on.

NORTHOVER FIRST SCHOOL - REVISED PRE-SCHOOL CLASS BUDGET

Number of children per year			24
LEA funding per child (capitation)			£1,000
Special needs budget			£0
Number of classes			1

	Notes	£	£
LEA funding			
Capitation			24,000
Special needs			-
Sub-total			24,000
Teaching staff			
Headmaster	1	-	
Playleader		15,000	
Sub-total			15,000
Ancilliary staff			
Secretary	2	-	
Caretaker	2	-	
Sub-total			-
Other costs			
Stationery	3	720	
Books and other resources	4	360	
IT support	5	1,000	
Heating	6	-	
Cleaning	6	-	
Maintenance	6	-	
Sundry	6	-	
Sub-total			2,080
Total costs			17,080
Contribution to fixed costs			6,920

Notes

1   The costs of the headteacher have been excluded because these are not marginal.

2   Apportionments of ancilliary staff costs have been excluded because they are not marginal.

3   The cost of stationery has been redrafted according to LEA guidelines. The fixed cost element has been excluded.

4   The cost of books and other resources has been redrafted according to LEA guidelines.

5   IT support has been included according to LEA guidelines.

6   Other costs that are not marginal have been excluded.

MEMO

Date: dd.mm.yy

To: Roger Austin
          Director of Education

From: Chetna Paul
          School Budget Co-ordinator

Subject: Extension of nursery provision

The attached schedule provides details of my calculations in arriving at an evaluation of the nursery class proposals. As you can see, at a session price of £4.50 per pupil, the proposals would generate additional revenue for the school's budget. However, if a choice had to be made between a pre-school for four year olds or a nursery class for three year olds in a purpose built unit, provision for four year olds would provide the greater financial benefit.

In answer to question 6, the calculations show that the majority of the costs of operating the nursery are fixed, with the exception of stationery and other resources, which amount to 75p per child per session. The net contribution per child to the fixed costs (£20,630) of the nursery is therefore £3.75 per session. If all the places are not filled, the contribution to fixed costs falls, and if only fourteen out of the eighteen places are taken up, the nursery would make a loss. Thus the key element to ensuring financial success is that all the places in the nursery are filled. If the session prices could be increased without affecting demand, then this would put the nursery class on a sounder financial footing.

On the issue of pricing, the calculations show that the project would breakeven at a session price of £3.69 per child. This is towards the lower end of the range that is currently charged in the private sector. We could therefore take a marginal cost plus pricing approach, whereby we add a profit margin to the breakeven price to arrive at the price to be charged. The calculations show that we could then respond to demand and to changing prices in the private sector, allowing us to achieve a reasonable contribution to the fixed costs of the school while ensuring that all the direct costs are covered.

A more traditional approach would be to use full cost plus pricing, whereby we allocate a full share of the school's overheads to the budget to arrive at the full cost of the class, and then add a profit mark-up on top. If we use this approach we are likely to arrive at a price which is uncompetitive with the private sector, since a school has a much higher level of overheads than does the average playgroup using space in a community building and having parent helpers.

I believe therefore that we should use a marginal cost plus approach, but take into account the level of demand for school nursery places and the private sector charges in order to maximise our revenue from the project.

1   NORTHOVER FIRST SCHOOL - NURSERY CLASS BUDGET

Number of children per session	18
Number of sessions per year (10 × 39)	390
Number of hours per year (10 × 390 × 3)	1,170

	£
Income (390 × 18 × £4.50)	**31,590**

Teaching staff:		
Playleader	14,000	
Assistant (1,170 × £4.50)	5,265	
Sub-total		19,265

Other costs:		
Stationery (390 × 18 × 50p)	3,510	
Other resources (390 × 18 × 25p)	1,755	
Extra heating & cleaning (39 × 5 × £7)	1,365	
Sub-total		6,630
Total costs		25,895
Annual revenue		5,695

2   For the class to **break even**, the **revenue** would have to be just sufficient to cover the **fixed costs**. In this case all the costs are effectively fixed, and therefore the annual revenue would have to be £25,895. The price at which the class would break even is therefore £25,895/390/18 = £3.69 per child per session.

3   The capital costs of undertaking the project are as follows.

	£	£
Building modifications:		
Cloakroom area	1,000	
Additional toilets	1,500	
Entrances and exits	1,500	
Fencing and security	3,000	
Sub-total		7,000
Equipment:		
Play equipment	3,000	
Furniture	2,500	
Sub-total		5,500
Total cost		12,500

The cost of redecoration has been excluded since this would be carried out in any case, and is not therefore required as a direct result of the project being undertaken.

Annual income from the project is £5,695. The payback period can be found as follow.

		£
Cumulative income at end of year	1	5,695
	2	11,390
	3	17,085

The project will therefore payback during year 3. The exact point can be estimated as (£12,500 – £11,390)/£5,695 = 0.2; therefore the payback period is 2.2 years.

4   *NPV analysis over five years*

	Year 0 £	Year 1 £	Year 2 £	Year 3 £	Year 4 £	Year 5 £
Building modifications	(7,000)					
Play equipment	(5,500)					
Revenue		5,695	5,696	5,695	5,695	5,695
Cash flow	(12,500)	5,695	5,695	5,695	5,695	5,695
15% discount factors	1.000	0.870	0.756	0.658	0.572	0.497
	£	£	£	£	£	£
PV of cash flow	(12,500)	4,955	4,305	3,747	3,258	2,830
Cumulative PV	(12,500)	(7,545)	(3,240)	507	3,765	6,595

The **NPV** benefit of the project over five years is £6,595.

5   In this situation, it appears that space is the **limiting factor**. The proposals for Northover show that a class of 24 four-year-olds produces a contribution to fixed costs of £6,920 per annum, or £288.33 per pupil. A class of 18 three-year-olds produces a contribution to fixed costs of £5,695 per annum, or £316.38 per pupil. In a purpose-built unit, the total contribution from the three-year-olds class containing 20 children would be £6,328, as compared with £6,920 from the four-year-olds class. Therefore a class of four-year-olds would give the greater financial benefit overall, despite the higher contribution per pupil from the three-year-olds class.

Task 4

MEMO

Date:	dd.mm.yy
To:	Sharon Coates Northover First School
From:	Chetna Paul Solent Local Education Authority
Subject:	Pre-school class financial evaluation

The budget for the pre-school class has been drawn up on the assumption that there is no alternative use for the classroom in question. If Mrs Parker is in favour of the use of the school by the toddler group at the price suggested, then this represents an alternative financial opportunity that would be foregone if the pre-school class is opened instead. The revenue that would be lost should therefore be charged to the pre-school class as an opportunity cost in the financial evaluation.

AAT SAMPLE SIMULATION

ANSWERS

Task 1

Analysis of costs

	Division C budget	Costs saved	Costs not saved
	£	£	£
Turnover	2,240,000		
Material	789,000	789,000	
Labour	524,100	524,100	
Light, heat and power	150,000		150,000
Rent	200,000		200,000
Rates	300,000		300,000
Sales commission	112,000	112,000	
Selling expenses	140,800	140,800	
Personnel	102,400		102,400
Finance	76,800		76,800
Administration	42,500		42,500
Loss	(197,600)	1,565,900	871,700

Change in profits

	£
Turnover lost if Division C is closed	2,240,000
Direct costs saved if Division C is closed	1,565,900
Contribution lost if Division C is closed	674,100

Recommendation

In the short term, Division C is contributing £674,100 to Questking's budgeted profit.

The costs saved if Division C is closed include not only the variable costs but also the direct fixed costs.

The central fixed overheads have been apportioned and so will still have to be met if the division was closed.

Closing the division down would cause profits to fall by the amount of its contribution.

It is therefore recommended that Division C is not closed in the short term.

Limitation to the recommendation (one example only)

There could be possible savings in some of the **central fixed overheads** such as depreciation or light, heat and power. However, the cost for the whole company for light, heat and power is only £440,000 which is less than the division's contribution.

In the short term it will not be possible to make savings in the cost of rent and rates. Over the longer term, it might be possible to rent out part of the factory or use the space occupied by Division C to develop a new division which would generate a larger contribution. Over the longer term, it might also be possible to reduce some of the central fixed overheads relating to personnel, finance and administration.

Task 2

Workings

Division B: Contribution per unit of limiting factor

	P1	P2	P3	P4
	£	£	£	£
Turnover	380,000	650,000	600,000	540,000
Material	114,000	195,000	120,000	180,000
Labour	45,600	93,600	144,000	27,000
Sales commission	19,000	32,500	30,000	27,000
Contribution	201,400	328,900	306,000	306,000
Sales volume	1,900	2,600	2,000	1,500
Contribution per unit	£106.00	£126.50	£153.00	£204.00
Material per unit (kg)	4.00	5.00	4.00	8.00
Contribution per kg	£26.50	£25.30	£38.25	£25.50
Order of preference	2	4	1	3

Revised production schedule

	Production units	Material used kg	Material balance kg	Unit contribution £	Total contribution £
Material available			26,800		
P3	2,000	8,000	18,800	153.00	306,000
P1	1,900	7,600	11,200	106.00	201,400
P4[1]	1,400	11,200	0	204.00	285,600
Revised contribution					793,000
Proposed contribution[2]					682,600
Increase in profit					110,400

Notes

1   11,200/8 = 1,400

2   Proposed contribution

	Production units	Unit contribution £	Total contribution £
P4	1,500	204.00	306,000
P2	2,600	126.50	328,900
P1	450	106.00	47,700
			682,600

A commercial limitation to the above analysis

The plan involves no production or sales of product P2 and only limited sales of product P4. This gap in the product range may cause customers to look elsewhere or tempt other suppliers to enter the market. These longer-term implications should, therefore, be considered before making a final decision.

Task 3

Calculation of existing fixed and variable costs of labour

	Quarter 1	Quarter 2	Quarter 3	Quarter 4
Units produced and sold	9,000	8,000	7,000	6,000
Labour (£)	97,500	92,000	86,500	81,000
Change in volume		−1,000	−1,000	−1,000
Change in labour cost (£)		−5,500	−5,500	−5,500
Piecework per unit (£)		5.50	5.50	5.50
Total cost of labour (£)	97,500	92,000	86,500	81,000
Total piecework cost (£)	49,500	44,000	38,500	33,000
Fixed cost of labour (£)	48,000	48,000	48,000	48,000

Calculation of existing quarterly cost of fixed production overheads

Annex 1.1		*or*	Annex 1.2	
Central overheads per year:	£		(Data for first quarter)	£
Light, heat and power	80,000		Fixed production overhead absorbed	36,000
Rent	50,000		Fixed production overhead unabsorbed	4,000
Rates	30,000		**Total per quarter**	40,000
Total	160,000			
Quarterly cost (£160,000/4)	£40,000			

Calculation of existing unit contribution

	Quarter 1
Units produced and sold	9,000
	£
Turnover	450,000
Material	198,000
Piecework cost of labour	49,500
Sales commission	22,500
Total contribution	180,000
Unit contribution (£)	20.00

Calculation of existing direct fixed costs

	£
Total fixed production overhead	40,000
Selling expenses	15,000
Labour fixed cost	48,000
Total direct fixed costs	103,000
Break-even point using existing direct fixed costs (£103,000/£20)	5,150

Break-even quarter

Quarter 1 of the following year

Calculation of revised unit contribution

	Quarter 1
Units produced and sold	9,000
	£
Turnover	450,000
Material	198,000
Piecework cost of labour	27,000
Sales commission	9,000
Total contribution	216,000
Unit contribution (£)	24.00

Calculation of revised direct fixed costs

	£
Total fixed production overhead	40,000
Selling expenses (£100,000/4)	25,000
Labour fixed cost (£280,000/4)	70,000
Total revised direct fixed costs	135,000
Break-even point using revised direct fixed costs (£135,000/£24)	5,625

Change in profit

Total contribution (30,000 × £20)	£600,000	Total contribution (30,000 × £24)	£720,000
Direct fixed costs (£103,000 × 4)	£412,000	Direct fixed costs (£135,000 × 4)	£540,000
Contribution	£188,000	Contribution	£180,000

Recommendation

Implementing the revised plan will reduce profits by £8,000 and is, therefore, not recommended, although the difference is relatively small. This apparent inconsistency arises because the proposed changes involve higher fixed costs which become more significant when volume decreases, as it does in quarters 2, 3 and 4.

Task 4

Calculation of maximum capacity

	£	Units
Total direct fixed production overhead absorbed in year	120,000	30,000
Overhead unabsorbed	40,000	
	160,000	

$\therefore$ 120,000/160,000 of capacity = 30,000 units

$\therefore$ Maximum capacity = $30,000 \times \dfrac{160,000}{120,000}$ = 40,000 units

$\therefore$ **Surplus capacity** = 10,000 units

Workings for special order

Existing marginal costs		£
Material	£198,000/9,000	22.00
Labour	£49,500/9,000	5.50
		27.50
Material saving		1.00
Revised marginal cost		26.50
Contract price		44.00
Unit contribution		17.50

MIDTOWN ENTERPRISE AGENCY

INTERNAL MEMO

Date: 1 December

To: Neil Henderson

From: Sally Parkin

Subject: Special order

As requested in your memo of 1 December, I have evaluated the three options. My detailed analysis is as follows.

Make all 12,000

	Units	£	£
Contribution	12,000	17.50	210,000
Contribution loss from existing sales	2,000	20.00	(40,000)
Opportunity cost of the additional material in stock	9,000		(36,000)
Cost of additional material purchased	3,000	18.00	(54,000)
Contribution			80,000

Make 10,000 and subcontract 2,000

	Units	£	£
Contribution on 10,000	10,000	17.50	175,000
Subcontract loss (Cost £46, selling price £44)	2,000	2.00	(4,000)
Opportunity cost of additional material in stock	9,000		(36,000)
Cost of additional material purchased	1,000	18.00	(18,000)
Contribution			117,000

Subcontract all 12,000

	Units	£	£
Loss on contract	12,000	2.00	24,000

On this basis I recommend that we manufacture 10,000 units and subcontract the extra 2,000 to Bright Processors Ltd.

Other issues (one only)

There are a number of non-financial issues which should be considered before accepting my recommendation, including the following.

- The possibility of Past Computers discovering that we are partly sourcing the contract from Bright Processors. Past Computers may decide to deal directly with Bright Processors.

- Uncertainty about the exact demand for the modems made by Division A. For example if demand was to fall by 2,000 compared to budget, the whole order could be sourced internally to give a contribution of £120,000.

Task 5

MIDTOWN ENTERPRISE AGENCY
INVESTMENT PROPOSAL

Calculation of operating cashflows

End of year	Demand units	Selling price	Cash received	Material unit	Material total	Labour unit	Labour total	Net cash flow
	a	b	c	d	e	f	g	h
			$a \times b$		$a \times d$		$a \times f$	$c - e - g$
1	8,000	120.00	960,000	60.00	480,000	20.00	160,000	320,000
2	8,000	96.00	768,000	48.00	384,000	20.60	164,800	219,200
3	8,000	76.80	614,400	38.40	307,200	21.22	169,760	137,440
4	8,000	61.44	491,520	30.72	245,760	21.86	174,880	70,880

Calculation of capital allowances

	£
Capital cost	480,000
Writing down allowance - year 1	120,000
Balance	360,000
Writing down allowance - year 2	90,000
Balance	270,000
Writing down allowance - year 3	67,500
Balance	202,500
Balancing allowance	202,500

Calculation of taxable profit

End of year	Profit before depreciation £	Capital allowances £	Taxable profit £	Corporation tax @ 30% £	Payable in year
1	320,000	120,000	200,000	60,000	2
2	219,200	90,000	129,200	38,760	3
3	137,440	67,500	69,940	20,982	4
4	70,880	202,500	(131,620)	(39,486)	5

Investment appraisal

End of year	Operating NCF £	Corporation tax £	Net cashflow £	25% factors	Discounted cashflow £
1	320,000		320,000	0.800	256,000
2	219,200	60,000	159,200	0.640	101,888
3	137,440	38,760	98,680	0.512	50,524
4	70,880	20,982	49,898	0.410	20,458
5		(39,486)	(39,486)	0.328	12,951
					441,821
Cost					480,000
NPV					(38,179)

Recommendation

With a negative **net present value**, the proposal should be rejected.

Justification of treatment of the £80,000 sales proceeds of existing machine ·

The sales proceeds from the existing machine are a **source of finance**. They do not reduce the real cost of the machine and so its capital cost remains at £480,000.

ORDER FORM

Any books from our AAT range can be ordered by telephoning 020-8740-2211. Alternatively, send this page to our address below, fax it to us on 020-8740-1184, or email us at **publishing@bpp.com.** Or look us up on our website: www.bpp.com

We aim to deliver to all UK addresses inside 5 working days; a signature will be required. Order to all EU addresses should be delivered within 6 working days. All other orders to overseas addresses should be delivered within 8 working days.

To: BPP Publishing Ltd, Aldine House, Aldine Place, London W12 8AW

Tel: 020-8740 2211   **Fax: 020-8740 1184**   **Email: publishing@bpp.com**

Mr / Ms (full name): _____

Daytime delivery address: _____

_____

Postcode: _____   Daytime Tel: _____

Please send me the following quantities of books.

	5/00 Interactive Text	8/00 DA Kit	8/00 CA Kit
FOUNDATION			
Unit 1 Recording Income and Receipts (7/00 Text)	☐	☐	
Unit 2 Making and Recording Payments (7/00 Text)	☐	☐	
Unit 3 Ledger Balances and Initial Trial Balance (7/00 Text)	☐		☐
Unit 4 Supplying information for Management Control (6/00 Text)	☐	☐	
Unit 20 Working with Information Technology (8/00 Text)	☐		
Unit 22/23 Achieving Personal Effectiveness (7/00) Text	☐		
INTERMEDIATE			
Unit 5 Financial Records and Accounts	☐		☐
Unit 6 Cost Information	☐		☐
Unit 7 Reports and Returns	☐	☐	
Unit 21 Using Information Technology	☐		
Unit 22: see below			
TECHNICIAN			
Unit 8/9 Core Managing Costs and Allocating Resources	☐		☐
Unit 10 Core Managing Accounting Systems	☐	☐	
Unit 11 Option Financial Statements (Accounting Practice)	☐		☐
Unit 12 Option Financial Statements (Central Government)	☐		☐
Unit 15 Option Cash Management and Credit Control	☐	☐	
Unit 16 Option Evaluating Activities	☐	☐	
Unit 17 Option Implementing Auditing Procedures	☐	☐	
Unit 18 Option Business Tax FA00(8/00 Text)	☐	☐	
Unit 19 Option Personal Tax FA00(8/00 Text)	☐		
TECHNICIAN 1999			
Unit 17 Option Business Tax Computations FA99 (8/99 Text & Kit)	☐	☐	
Unit 18 Option Personal Tax Computations FA99 (8/99 Text & Kit)	☐	☐	
TOTAL BOOKS	☐ +	☐ + ☐ =	☐

Postage and packaging: @ £9.95 each = £ ☐
UK: £2.00 for each book to maximum of £10
Europe (inc ROI and Channel Islands): £4.00 for first book, £2.00 for each extra   P & P   £ ☐
Rest of the World: £20.00 for first book, £10 for each extra

► Unit 22 Maintaining a Healthy Workplace Interactive Text (postage free)   ☐   @ £3.95   £ ☐

GRAND TOTAL   £ ☐

I enclose a cheque for £ _____ (cheques to BPP Publishing Ltd) or charge to Mastercard/Visa/Switch

Card number ☐☐☐☐ ☐☐☐☐ ☐☐☐☐ ☐☐☐☐ ☐☐☐☐

Start date _____   Expiry date _____   Issue no. (Switch only)___

Signature _____